PAUSE AND REFLECT

By

Shweta Kulkarni

The First Volume of Mindful Lifestyle Blueprint for the Modern World

Inspired from Podcast - Take A Pause with Shweta & Sudeep

Words of Appreciation for Pause and Reflect

"*Mindfulness is the cornerstone of impactful leadership and authentic public speaking. In Pause and Reflect, Shweta Kulkarni knits the power of self-awareness and presence into a guide that inspires readers to lead with clarity and communicate with purpose. This book is a must-read for everyone striving to connect deeply with themselves and their audience.*"

- Dr. Divya Jaitly, Award Winning Entrepreneur, Motivational Speaker & Author of 'Beyond The Pitch'

"*Life's intense examinations truly begin after graduation. The stories in Pause and Reflect serve as exemplary guides for driving a successful life. My generation found inspiration and wisdom in the timeless tales of Panchatantra, Akbar-Birbal, and Ramayana. In today's digital era, we need daily detox practices and mindful tips to maintain peace and achieve success simultaneously. This book is a MUST-READ for everyone seeking harmony in modern life.*" **-
Ramesh Joshi, Founder & Director of Nichrome, India**

"*Pause & Reflect is nothing short of a well-nourished plate of nutrition for both the mind and the soul. Through its captivating stories, pearls of wisdom, heartfelt emotions, and practical tips, Shweta invites readers to embark on a profound journey of mindfulness. Her expertise in this domain shines effortlessly through each story, offering both depth and relatability. It is not just a collection of stories; it's a gospel of mindful living, a gentle reminder to pause, reflect, and rediscover the magic within and around you.*" -
Mehernosh Randeria, NLP Master Trainer and Coach

"*As a director, I've learned the value of taking a moment to pause and reflect before making key decisions. In Pause and Reflect, Shweta Kulkarni shows us how mindfulness can be our guiding light, not just in our careers, but in every area of life. This book is an empowering journey of self-discovery that teaches us to align our actions with our* deeper purpose. Highly recommended for everyone to lead a life with greater clarity and peace." - **Umesh Kulkarni, Movie Director**

"In my journey as a Bikini Pro, I've learned that physical results come when the mind is calm and focused. Pause and Reflect aligns perfectly with this philosophy, teaching us how mindfulness helps us achieve greatness in the gym and in life. Just as Lord Krishna guides Arjuna in the Bhagavad Gita to focus on the process, not just the outcome. This book teaches us to stay grounded and aware in every step of our journey. It's not about perfection; it's about mindful progress. This is a must-read for everyone looking to elevate their body and mind to achieve optimum results" - **Sarina Pani, IFBB Bikini Pro and Fitness coach**

'Pause And Reflect' is a beautiful blend of wisdom and practicality, offering powerful stories and actionable tips to help us embrace mindfulness in our daily lives. Through simple yet profound insights, it gently reminds us to be present, find joy in the now, and live with greater awareness. A must-read for all to cultivate a more peaceful and fulfilling life. - **Dr. Meenu Singh, Author of 'The Intentional Daughter-In Law' & Personal Empowerment Coach**

In an era where the pace of life often feels relentless and the demands unending, Shweta Kulkarni offers us a profound gift of 'Pause and Reflect.' This book is more than a guide, it is a companion, thoughtfully crafted to help readers find clarity and purpose amidst the noise. Through timeless stories and actionable mindfulness insights, Shweta invites us to step back, breathe, and rediscover the simple yet transformative power of presence. I am confident this book is a must read for all age groups and will inspire countless people to embrace a more mindful and meaningful approach to life. - **Prashant Ranade, Technology Evangelist**

Table of Contents

Author's Note – How to Make the Best Use of This Book

Back in 2022, as we were all recovering from the pandemic, I noticed something within all of us. While physical fitness took a hit due to restricted access to gyms and outdoor activities, it was our mental health that truly suffered. As social beings, we were forced into isolation due to strict no-touch policies, and the only way to stay connected was through digital means.

One day, amid this post-pandemic chaos, my husband Sudeep and I were having coffee at our favorite hotel, Roopali, on FC Road in Pune, India. I said, "Sudeep, all we hear these days is negativity, through the news, social media, everywhere. What if we start something positive and empowering for people who listen to it?" He asked what I had in mind, and I said, "Let's start a podcast."

Sudeep, with his background in theater, direction, and anchoring since college, has an incredible gift for storytelling - when he speaks, people listen. Meanwhile, during the pandemic, I had earned my Mindfulness Coach certification and was deeply inspired by the tools and concepts it offered. We decided to merge our strengths - Sudeep would narrate a story, and I would share insights on applying mindfulness in different areas of life. That's how *Take A Pause with Shweta and Sudeep* was born, finally launching in April 2023.

With our existing work commitments, we approached it as a passion project, setting a goal of at least 100 episodes before deciding whether to continue. And here it is - our podcast, a space for meaningful conversations and mindful reflections.

This podcast became my inspiration to write my first book. *Pause and Reflect* is a collection of stories spanning different eras and inspired by various authors. I encourage you to pause while reading these short yet impactful stories, taking a few moments to reflect on their mindful insights. This book is not just a one-time read, whenever you open it, no matter where you are in life, it can serve as a companion, like a coach guiding you out of stuck situations or helping you progress in different aspects of life.

In today's fast-paced world, where distractions are constant and expectations relentless, mindfulness offers a way to reconnect with ourselves, rediscover balance, and live with intention. To me, mindfulness isn't just a practice; it's a way of life. It has transformed how I approach challenges, embrace growth, and move through each day with clarity and purpose. Through this book, especially the *Mindful Reflections* section, I share everything I have learned and wish to offer.

Pause and Reflect is also a reflection of my personal journey as a trainer, speaker, and coach. It's an invitation to slow down, tune in, and explore the profound simplicity of the present moment. Legends like Buddha, Thich Nhat Hanh, Prem Rawat, Ellen Langer, Eckhart Tolle, and many other great authors have spoken about awareness, being present, accepting the past while envisioning the future, and the infinite opportunities that lie ahead. Most importantly, they emphasize self-discovery - knowing oneself deeply. In my own way, here I am joining this incredible movement of Mindfulness Advocates.

One of the most powerful aspects of mindfulness that resonated with me is self-acceptance. It teaches us to embrace ourselves completely - our emotions, both high and low, our physical appearance, and every aspect of who we are. For me, mindfulness has been a tool not just for personal growth but also for enhancing my relationships, career, and overall well-being. I invite you into this space, free of resistance and opposition, to discover your own path.

This book isn't a set of rules or instructions - it's a collection of reflections, tools, and practices that I hope will inspire you to pause, reflect, and create a more intentional, fulfilling life. Mindfulness isn't about perfection; it's about presence. As you turn these pages, I encourage you to embark on this journey with curiosity and an open heart. Let's explore how mindfulness can help you travel through life's complexities while embracing its beauty.

Acknowledgment

Writing Pause and Reflect has been a deeply transformative journey, one that demanded dedication, discipline, and unshakable consistency. No matter how brilliant our ideas may be, their accomplishment depends on focus and commitment. This book is a testament to that truth, and I am profoundly grateful to everyone who walked this path with me.

To my family - my dear husband, Sudeep, thank you for everything and everything you do for me, your support has been priceless to me and my beautiful daughter, Swara - thank you for your endless love and always mentioning how proud you always have been of me. Your belief in me, especially in moments when you both said, "You got this," gave me the strength to turn this dream into reality. You stood by me through restless nights, countless revisions, and my anxious deadlines, and for that, I am eternally grateful.

My heartfelt gratitude to the world class brand that has been an integral part of my journey for over a decade - ZUMBA. To the incredible ZHO team, whose consistent support and appreciation have helped me grow into a better version of myself with every training I taught.

A special thanks to my Mindfulness teachers, Karan Behl and Pravin Chaturvedi, whose wisdom and guidance have shaped my practice. To my ICF coaching programs' trainer, Anil Dagia, for his invaluable insights that refined my coaching journey. And to my book coach, Heena Shrivastava - your mentorship has been truly transformative. Heena, you not only taught me the art of writing a book but also helped shape my scattered thoughts into a work I felt confident and proud to publish. Your mantra, "Never doubt yourself, take one step at a time," will always resonate with me.

To my dearest friend, Dr. Meenu Singh, thank you for your selfless support and constant inspirational words. Your debut book, The Intentional Daughter-In-Law, is an incredible read, and your encouragement came as a gift when I needed it most.

I am forever grateful to my parents, whose love and values have shaped the person I am today. A heartfelt thank you to my father-in-law, whose endless enthusiasm and support have been truly inspiring. And to you, the reader - thank you for picking up Pause and Reflect. It's an honor to be a part of your journey. I hope these pages inspire you to PAUSE, REFLECT, and discover the clarity, peace, and purpose that mindfulness brings.

Mindfully yours,
Shweta Kulkarni

Foreword

A father gave the job of painting their home to his 12 years old son. "My strong boy, would you paint our house by the evening? I will come back from work by then." Father's voice was warm. Son nodded to affirm. When the father returned in the evening, his eyes sparkled with joy and satisfaction, seeing the porch and front-yard being painted so meticulously. Each stroke of brush seemed like a painting. In fact, the colour combo taken was also something he could never imagine that his son had a sense of.

However, as he strode inside, he noticed that there was nothing done inside the home. He camouflaged his disappointment in a gulp and asked son the reason for not painting it from inside.

The son replied, "Dad, come on! Who is looking from inside. Everyone sees it from outside only." Father instantly replied, "Well, no one EXCEPT US is looking from inside."

Shweta's "Pause & Reflect" is one such leakproof, power-packed tool which will help you to not just look within but refill the colour in your life's narratives.

I believe firmly that Coaching is the journey and learning is the destination for both the coach and the coachee. While Shweta was writing this book under my guidance and support, I realized that there were few things which were a game changer which stood out in Shweta. The first being, she lives up to her name, which means whiteness, or brightness. When there will be darkness all around, Shweta will be the one standing with tiniest matchstick and being happy about the light source. Her outlook to choose brightness reflects in each word she has carefully crafted in this book.

In short, a caution for the readers – THIS BOOK WILL CHANGE YOUR MINDSET (in a good way for sure). The question here is – Are you ready to change or will some change make you ready?

Heena M Shrivastava,
Author of 4 books, Book Writing Coach,
ICF-PCC, Certified NLP trainer, Tedx Speaker

"Do not dwell in the past, do not dream
of the future, concentrate the mind on
the present moment." - Buddha

Did Even Gods Know the Purpose of Their Lives?

It was a sultry afternoon in the grand city of Ayodhya, where the palace was alive with the sounds of lunch preparations. The aroma of exquisite dishes filled the air, but King Dashrath barely noticed. As he entered the dining hall, Queen Kausalya waited eagerly, hoping for a word of praise for the culinary feast. But today, the King was not his usual self. Lost in thought, he absently toyed with the food on his plate with a mask of worry on his face.

"O King Dashrath, what's the matter? Does the food not please you?" Kausalya's voice trembled slightly as she asked the question, her heart sinking as she saw the distant look in her husband's eyes.

King Dashrath, startled from his thoughts, looked up. "Oh, dear Kausalya, no, it's not the food," he replied, his voice heavy with emotion. But even as he spoke, he couldn't meet her gaze. His brow was furrowed with deep lines of worry, leaving Kausalya in a state of quiet concern. She chose to wait, sensing that there was more on his mind than what was meeting the eye.

After a long silence, Dashrath finally spoke, his voice breaking, "What is the use of all this royal splendour when I have no heir to inherit it? It will all be lost the day I breathe my last." His eyes welled up with tears, and he looked away, struggling to contain his emotions.

Kausalya watched as her husband's mind seemed to drift far away, his lips moving silently as if in conversation with some unseen force. In that moment, Dashrath was transported back to the darkest day of his life. The memory of a tragic mistake haunted him. The picture of his fiercely shot arrow thrashing into the chest of a young lad, Shravan flashed and tears rolled down his cheeks.

"Oh King! You killed my son! I curse you, just like us, you too will die grieving for a son." Shravan's father, who was shattered into pieces after witnessing his son's body, spat the curse through his words.

The weight of those words pierced inside him like the pain of an arrow, causing an excruciating agony that had never fully left him. He had begged for forgiveness, knowing it was a terrible mistake, but the curse remained. And now, as the years passed, he realised with growing dread that for the curse to come true, he must first have a son - a hope that seemed more distant with each passing day.

Ayodhya, the capital of the kingdom of Kosala, was a city of peace and prosperity, ruled by the wise and just King Dashrath. The people loved their king, and crime was almost unknown in the city. Yet, a shadow loomed over Ayodhya, as Dashrath constantly worried about who would succeed him on the throne. He had a daughter, Shanta, who was married to the sage Rishyasringa, but no sons to carry on his legacy. His three wives - Kausalya, Kaikeyi, and Sumitra - shared in his concern, for the absence of a male heir weighed heavily on the hearts of Ayodhya's citizens as well.

Determined to break free from this curse and secure an heir, King Dashrath made a decision. He would perform the Putreshti Yagna, a powerful sacrificial ceremony to seek the blessings of the gods for a son. It was decided that Sage Rishyasringa would conduct the yagna and as the preparations began, the air in the palace buzzed with anticipation.

As the ceremony commenced, the chanting of mantras filled the air, invoking Lord Indra. But in the heavens, turmoil reigned. Indra had recently lost a battle against the demon-king Ravana, who had turned the earth into a realm of chaos and suffering. Desperate for a solution, Indra approached Brahma, the creator, who admitted his hands were tied by a boon he had granted Ravana, making the demon invincible to gods. Brahma advised Indra to seek help from Vishnu, the preserver.

Vishnu, who has always been considered wise and strategic, assured Indra that Ravana's boon had a loophole - he was not protected from men or animals. "I will be born as a man to bring about Ravana's death," Vishnu declared, hinting that the wheels of fate were already in motion.

As the Putreshti Yagna reached its climax, a miraculous event unfolded. A celestial being appeared before the king, bearing a golden bowl filled with divine pudding. The deity instructed Dashrath to distribute the pudding among his wives to fulfil his wish for sons. With hope rekindled, Dashrath gave half of the pudding to Kausalya, his eldest queen and divided the remaining half between Sumitra and Kaikeyi.

Yet, fate had one more twist in store. The remnants of the divine pudding were accidentally left among the utensils to be washed. A crow, drawn by the divine scent, snatched the bowl and flew far away, eventually settling atop a hill in Kishkindha, the land of monkeys. There, the bowl slipped from the crow's grasp and rolled down the hill, where it was discovered by a huge monkey named Kesari. He took it to his wife, Anjana, who ate the leftover pudding.

Soon, Ayodhya was filled with joyous news - the queens were expecting children. On the ninth day of the month of Chaitra, Kausalya gave birth to a son, Rama. The entire city erupted in celebration, rejoicing at the birth of their future king. Shortly after, Kaikeyi and Sumitra also gave birth to sons, while in Kishkindha, Anjana gave birth to a mighty monkey named Hanuman.

Thirteen days later, the grand naming ceremony was held. The revered sage Vashishta bestowed the name Rama, meaning "the pleasant one," upon Kausalya's son. And so, the divine avatar of Vishnu was born into the world, destined to bring peace and prosperity to the earth and to end Ravana's reign of terror. But as the infant Rama lay in his mother's arms, the question lingered - did he know the purpose for which he was born? Only time would reveal the true path he was destined to walk, a path of heroism, sacrifice, and the fulfilment of a destiny that would change the world forever.

(This story is inspired by the works of author Sunita Pant Bansal. We do not claim any copyright or credits for it.)

Mindful Reflections :

Just like Lord Rama, we are all born with a purpose. Imagine if the gods sent us into the world with a stamp or tattoo that clearly indicated our reason for existence - what a funny thought, right? Yet, even the greatest monks meditating in the Himalayas have acknowledged that understanding our purpose can take a lifetime.

In today's world, the idea of "Purposeful Living" is highly cherished. But why do so many life coaches, psychologists and philanthropists emphasise the importance of finding our purpose to lead happier lives?

Let's start by understanding life - it's an ongoing journey, not a destination. Life, in its simplest form, is the journey from birth to death. But defining it this way feels uninspiring, doesn't it? As we navigate through this journey, we need motivation, support and a solid reason to feel useful to ourselves and the world. This desire to feel important, appreciated and empowered builds our self-esteem and self-belief, leading to a confident and fulfilling life. Living with purpose means living at our best potential.

But don't let the concept of purposeful living overwhelm you. Let's simplify it - Purposeful living is found in our everyday actions - what we do, why we do it and how long we choose to do it. How do you discover what you love to do? This process of understanding what we love makes us unique and is also a journey of self-discovery. Each aspect of life - self, relationships, career - carries its own purpose. There isn't just one single purpose in life. Knowing your values, principles, interests, and beliefs guides you to take meaningful actions. While your values and interests might remain constant for a while, your beliefs around your values will evolve. All your successful moments are driven by your strong beliefs as only your beliefs make you take all actions.

To know yourself better, practice self-awareness daily. Morning meditations are a powerful way to connect with yourself. Sit quietly, focus on your breath, inhale and exhale and let your thoughts flow without resistance. As you become more self-aware, you'll understand your values and interests, guiding you to take actions that either monetize your interests or simply bring you joy.

Remember, not every interest needs to be monetized. The greatest benefit of following your passions is that whenever you face a downfall, your intrinsic motivation will help you rise again because your "why" is significant to you. Purposeful living is the key to a happier and wealthier life. Every breath is a fresh start, my dear learners. If you're reading this, be thankful because 'You are Alive'. Take action today!

❖ ❖ ❖

"Mindfulness is the simple act of actively noticing things." - Ellen Langer

Greed and Gold both are useless, would you agree?

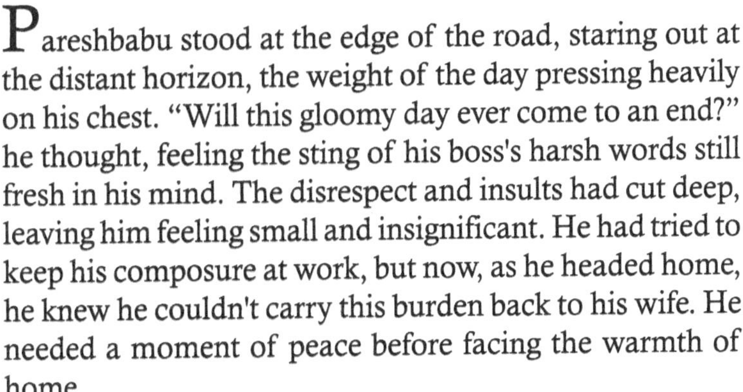

Pareshbabu stood at the edge of the road, staring out at the distant horizon, the weight of the day pressing heavily on his chest. "Will this gloomy day ever come to an end?" he thought, feeling the sting of his boss's harsh words still fresh in his mind. The disrespect and insults had cut deep, leaving him feeling small and insignificant. He had tried to keep his composure at work, but now, as he headed home, he knew he couldn't carry this burden back to his wife. He needed a moment of peace before facing the warmth of home.

He decided to stop by the beach, hoping the sound of the waves and the expanse of the ocean might soothe his troubled mind. The beach had always been his sanctuary, a place where he could think clearly and find some solace since his childhood. But today, as he walked toward the shore, something felt different.

The beach was quiet, uncanny, as if it too was holding its breath, waiting for something to happen. The waves, usually so lively and full of energy, seemed hollow, retreating into themselves each time they lapped at the shore. It was as though the ocean was drawing back, swallowing its own waters, leaving the beach bare and desolate.

Pareshbabu noticed this change immediately. Just last week, he had visited this very spot with his wife. The waves had been playful then, dancing around their feet as they laughed, their hearts were lit with joy. But today, the ocean seemed distant, as if it was pulling away from him just as he tried to approach it.

He walked closer, but with each step he took, the waves receded further, disappearing into the deep, dark belly of the sea. The once comforting sound of the water had turned into an echoing silence, amplifying the loneliness he felt inside.

Pareshbabu sighed deeply, realising that the peace he sought wouldn't be found here today. The beach, like his own spirit, was emptied, waiting for something to fill it once more. He stood there for a long time, watching the waves draw further away, feeling the emptiness stretch out before him, as vast as the ocean itself.

And yet, in that moment of hollow retreat, a memory from his childhood suddenly washed over him, splashing into his mind like a wave against the shore. He looked down at the sand and pebbles beneath his feet, remembering how, as a child, he had loved playing with the ocean's pebbles, filling his pockets with them and carrying them home. It was a simple act, but it had brought him happiness, a sense of contentment that seemed so distant now.

Pondering this memory, Pareshbabu slowly sank down onto the sand and began to gather pebbles in his big manly hands. He carefully selected the ones that caught his eye, the ones that reminded him of those carefree childhood days and placed them in his pockets. Each pebble seemed to carry a piece of that lost joy, a fragment of the peace he had come here to find.

With his pockets filled, he stood up and took one last look at the retreating ocean. The emptiness he had felt earlier still lingered, but it was now mingled with a quiet resolve. He turned and headed home, ready to face whatever lay ahead, knowing that filling his pockets with pebbles had also filled a small part of the void within him. Just as these pebbles brought a hint of positivity to Pareshbabu, he realised that even small, seemingly insignificant actions could help restore his sense of peace.

After a long walk, he reached home, where his wife was. Subhadra was waiting for him. After freshening up, Pareshbabu went to his study, removed those ocean pebbles & stones from his pocket and placed it on his desk. He also removed his silver-coloured wristwatch and set it near the stones and pebbles. Then, he pulled out some books from his cupboard and strolled around the room with one in hand.

As he was about to start reading again, he noticed something strange. His wristwatch had turned yellow! Shocked and surprised, he clearly remembered that his watch was silver. How could it have turned yellow?

Pareshbabu examined everything kept on that table carefully. The watch had only been near those stones and pebbles he had collected from his ocean stroll. Now when he observed more carefully he noticed a shining stone in those bunch of stones and pebbles which looked greenish with no polish on either side with slightly sharp edges. Intrigued, he placed the stone on one of his shirts and watched carefully, but nothing happened. Doubting himself for a moment, he opened the door latch with his left hand, in which he held the stone. To his astonishment, the rusted iron latch turned yellow.

Pareshbabu couldn't believe his eyes. He realised the stone was no ordinary stone; it was a 'Parees' - a rare stone that could turn iron into gold. Many wars had been fought over Parees in early human civilizations, but it had been extinct for ages. Pareshbabu's mind raced with the possibilities. With this stone, he could become the richest person on the planet. He could turn every object made of iron into gold and sell it. Despite knowing Subhadra had a big mouth, he couldn't control his excitement in telling his wife about the stone, making her vow to keep it a secret.

Pareshbabu was smart enough to use this opportunity to brighten up his gloomy life from all the distress he was getting from his workplace. The first thing he did was resign from his existing job and bought a small workshop that dealt in heavy, rusted iron and began using the stone to turn everything into gold. As his sales skyrocketed, he started to mint money. Neighbours were astonished and assumed Pareshbabu had come into a gifted wealth. When questioned, he remained silent. Within two years, he was one of the richest men in the world.

As his wealth grew, Pareshbabu knew he needed a trustworthy assistant to manage his factory. After interviewing thousands of candidates, he met Matthew, a young man who was lame, in love and without obsessions. Matthew was happy with the small salary Pareshbabu offered and never questioned how iron was converted to gold. He spent his days at the factory and evenings with Menka, the love of his life. For Matthew, money never equaled happiness.

Pareshbabu received invitations from many countries to share his formula for creating gold. Beautiful women wrote letters, praising and proposing to him, which Subhadra, agitated, handled. Pareshbabu maintained good relations with the government, ministers, and influential people, which helped him dodge allegations. Many scientists tried to uncover his secret, but found nothing suspicious. However, as time passed, envy grew and Pareshbabu started receiving death threats. Some people saw him as a monster who could disrupt the world order, leading to protests against him.

One day, Subhadra said, "Pareshbabu, we have enough wealth to last a lifetime. We have no children, and I don't want to live in fear. This stone has brought us wealth but also made our lives a living hell. Let's throw it away and go on a pilgrimage to Kashi." Pareshbabu, wise and needing this nudge, agreed.

He called Matthew and said, "Matthew, I want this stone destroyed completely. No one should ever find it." Matthew, obedient and loyal as ever, took the stone, ensuring Pareshbabu not to worry.

That night, Pareshbabu's manager came running to him, saying, "Pareshbabu, Matthew sir has gone mad. He's crying and trying to commit suicide." Pareshbabu rushed to Matthew, who sobbed, "Menka is marrying someone else. Her father refuses me because I lack wealth and I am Christian while they are Hindu. I can't live without her and want to end my life with these cyanide tablets."

Pareshbabu asked about the stone. Matthew said, "I swallowed it. Now it can never be found. It will stay in my body, and when I die, it will be destroyed with me." Pareshbabu thought for a moment and said, "Okay. I will make sure you marry Menka. Don't worry; I'll handle this."

Pareshbabu called Menka's father and revealed the stone's whereabouts. He promised Matthew would convert to Hinduism. Menka's father, enticed by the wealth, agreed. They took Matthew to a doctor, who confirmed the stone's presence in his intestine. The doctor assured it wouldn't harm Matthew.

Menka married Matthew after he embraced Hinduism, believing that their love would carry them through any challenges. In the early months of their marriage, they were happy, enjoying the simplicity of life and the comfort of each other's company. Matthew felt fulfilled, grateful that he had found love and the family life he had always longed for. The dark thoughts that once haunted him, including thoughts of suicide, seemed to fade into the background.

However, as time passed, Menka began to change. What had once been a shared dream of a simple, loving family life was overshadowed by Menka's growing ambition. She became increasingly preoccupied with wealth and status, dreaming of a life filled with luxury rather than the modest happiness they had built together. Her excitement for material success overshadowed her commitment to their marriage, and Matthew, who had always valued love over riches, started to feel the distance between them grow.

Six months into their marriage, Menka discovered she was pregnant. Matthew was overjoyed, his heart swelling with love at the thought of becoming a father. He saw the baby as the ultimate symbol of their union, the next chapter in their life together. But Menka's reaction was starkly different. She wasn't pleased with the news, seeing the pregnancy as an obstacle to her plans of wealth and social status. Her growing ambition left little room for the idea of motherhood and soon, she made a decision that shattered Matthew's world.

Without Matthew's consent, Menka aborted the baby. The decision broke Matthew's heart, leaving him devastated. The one thing he had cherished most - love and the dream of a family - was torn away from him. As the reality of the situation set in, everything between them began to unravel. Matthew realised that Menka no longer loved him, that her ambitions had taken precedence over their relationship.

A year later, the final blow came. Menka's father, furious over the dissolution of a precious stone, the Parees stone, in Matthew's stomach, accused him of deceit and demanded a divorce. Menka, who was by now fully consumed by her own aspirations, agreed without hesitation. In the wake of these events, all the gold that

Pareshbabu had converted reverted back to iron, as if to signify the futility of their greed.

Despite the chaos and heartbreak, Matthew found an unexpected sense of peace. He had come to terms with what had happened, accepting that life must move forward. He remembered the teachings of Swami Vivekananda: "Greed and Gold are both worthless." This wisdom resonated with him deeply and he chose to let go of his past, embracing the present and the possibilities it held.

Matthew continued working in Pareshbabu's factory, earning the same modest salary, but with a newfound sense of contentment. Free from the weight of Menka's ambitions and the turmoil of the past, he found solace in the simplicity of his daily routines and the small joys that life offered. In the end, Matthew realised that true wealth wasn't in gold, riches or relying on others for fulfilment. Instead, it was in the peace that comes from accepting life as it is and finding contentment within oneself.

(This story is inspired by the works of author Satyajit Ray. We do not claim any copyright or credits for it.)

Mindful Reflections: 》》

In today's world, money, wealth, gold and riches are unquestionably crucial for maintaining a comfortable lifestyle. They provide security, opportunities and a certain level of comfort. Yet, it's equally essential to recognize the true wealth of human life - things that cannot be bought with money. This includes the love of those around us, the joy we share with friends and family and the peace and satisfaction within ourselves. The true richness of life is found in balancing three key areas – self (mental health & physical health), relationships and career/finance.

A fulfilling life requires a balance between self-fulfilment, healthy relationships and career achievements. If any of these areas are out of sync, life may feel incomplete. Self-fulfilment comes from personal growth and understanding one's purpose. Relationships involve nurturing connections with loved ones, friends and family, which are sources of happiness and self-esteem. Career and financial stability provide the means to live comfortably, pursue dreams and live the purpose of this one life we have. Achieving equilibrium in these areas can lead to a more satisfying and content life.

But have you already thought about this – while acquiring wealth is important, the journey and process of earning it plays a significant role in shaping our character. It's not just about the destination but also about how we get there. The path we take to achieve our goals builds our character and teaches us the value of hard work, integrity and respect for what we earn. Acknowledging and appreciating this journey helps us maintain a healthier perspective on wealth and success. Greed is often a subtle, yet powerful force that can distort our values and priorities. It's essential to be aware of this thin line between seeking wealth and succumbing to greed. Greed is considered one of life's most destructive sins and while it's common to have desires, it's crucial to recognize when these desires cross into unhealthy territory. Greed can lead to neglecting what truly matters – our loved ones and our sense of fulfilment. Keeping greed in check ensures that we do not lose sight of what is genuinely important in life.

> With these lessons in mind, I invite you to take a moment to reflect on what truly matters to you. Write down the first five things that come to mind – these could be people, values, experiences or aspects of your life that bring you joy and fulfilment. There is no right or wrong answer; the exercise is about acknowledging what you genuinely value. Overcoming the resistance conditioned by upbringing or societal influences allows you to reconnect with what is most important in your life. In this journey of balancing wealth with what matters most, remember – the best quality of life is achieved when we harmonise self-fulfilment, relationships and financial stability, while respecting the path we take and guarding against the perils of greed because as Swami Vivekananda once said "Greed and Gold are both worthless."

❖ ❖ ❖

"You can't stop the waves, but you can learn to surf." - Jon Kabat-Zinn

Do you see that 'Ray of Light' at the end of the dark tunnel?

Rajesh had barely been at work for two hours when he found himself mindlessly scrolling through Instagram, eyes glued to the travel pages that always made his heart flutter. Rajesh deeply loved exploring new places, the thrill of adventure and the peace of relaxing in nature. Today, his workload was light, unlike his colleague Rohan, seated just across from him, buried under a mountain of tasks.

"Rajesh," Rohan whispered, careful not to draw too much attention, "Are you lost on Instagram again? You must have a lot of free time!" He tossed a stack of papers onto Rajesh's desk, adding, "Help me finish these, will you? I have a deadline before lunch."

Feeling slightly guilty, Rajesh agreed and got to work on Rohan's task. After finishing the work, the two headed to the canteen together. As they walked, Rajesh's phone buzzed. He glanced at the screen and hesitated, eyebrows furrowed. Rohan noticed and gave him a questioning look, asking non-verbally, "Who is it?"

Once they found a table in the crowded canteen, Rajesh picked up the call. "Hello Ma, how are you?" he greeted, slipping into his routine chat with his mother. Lately, his mother had been calling almost daily during lunch, urging him to visit home. She missed him, she said, as it had been ages since he last visited their small village in North India. And, of course, there was the ever-present topic of marriage.

"Rajesh, beta," she would say, "You're not getting any younger. Get married this year, or there won't be any girls left who'll accept you. Today's educated girls want young, handsome, rich boys settled in big cities like Mumbai. So hurry up and get married. I'll feel like I've fulfilled another responsibility, just like when you completed your engineering and got that job in Mumbai."

Her words lingered in Rajesh's mind, even as Rohan tried to show him something on his phone. He was lost in thoughts about his mother's longing, the expectations of marriage and the growing emptiness he felt despite his comfortable life in Mumbai. Rohan eventually snapped him out of it with a light pat on the arm.

"Rohan, these pictures are amazing!" Rajesh exclaimed when he finally looked at the screen. "I just saw mountains like these on Instagram earlier. Where have you been?"

"Last month, I went trekking in Leh-Ladakh," Rohan began, his eyes lighting up as he recounted the trip. "Rajesh, you know I'm still single, but this trip was incredible. I met many people like me, exploring life on their terms. But the beauty of the place it's beyond words. It felt like I was in a dream, not just looking at pictures on a screen."

Rajesh felt a pang of envy and longing. Here he was, working at a prestigious IT company in Mumbai, drawing a handsome salary and living a stable, predictable life. But suddenly, the same routine that had once felt secure now seemed suffocating. That evening, he went home feeling unusually gloomy, his thoughts consumed by memories of his mother's words and Rohan's scenic adventure. Sleep eluded him as he tossed and turned, haunted by a deep sense of FOMO - fear of missing out on life's travel adventures.

The next day at the office, Rajesh braced himself for another dull day. But as he sifted through his inbox, something unusual caught his eye - an email from the company's CSR head. It was an invitation to visit a remote village in Northeast India, an all-expenses-paid trip with a 90-day paid leave. He re-read the email twice, thinking there must be a catch. And there it was - Teach Basic Hindi to the village kids.

A spark ignited in his eyes the third time he read the email. "Paid leave? Seriously? Who wouldn't jump at this chance?" he thought, nearly leaping out of his chair in excitement. Convincing his boss was easier than he'd imagined. It seemed like he got a green light amidst the heavy traffic of his thoughts. Rajesh couldn't wait to share the news with Rohan.

"Listen, bro," he began, his voice buzzing excitedly, "Starting today, I'm on a three-month paid leave. I'll still get my full salary just for teaching Hindi. Your boy is about to live it up!" Rohan's face lit up with happiness for his friend and they exchanged a celebratory high-five. In his mind, Rajesh was already picturing himself sipping tea in the heart of nature, somewhere peaceful in Northeast India, far removed from the daily grind and even closer to his hometown.

The next day, he booked a flight, daydreaming about his luxurious escape and the chance to see his family. As the plane touched down, he was greeted by a breathtaking view - clouds hanging low over a tiny airstrip between towering mountain ranges. "What a view!" he thought, snapping a quick photo. But his idyllic fantasy began to crack as a small, rickety jeep appeared to take him on the 100-kilometre journey to the village - a journey that would take eight long, gruelling hours on what could barely be called a road.

When he finally arrived, exhausted and covered in dust, the village greeted him with an eerie silence. The villagers stared at him as if he were an alien who had just descended from a UFO. Feeling awkward, he approached one of them and asked, "Where is the school?" The man stared blankly. He tried again with the postman, who looked like he'd been asked to donate a kidney. Finally, the driver who had brought him there explained, "No one here speaks Hindi."

Rajesh was stunned. How could an entire village in India not speak the country's official language? The next day, he found the school, a modest building with just one teacher and about a hundred kids. His company had sponsored the Hindi program, and so he began teaching. But the challenge was far more significant than he had anticipated. Days turned into weeks, and no matter how hard he tried, the kids couldn't grasp even the language basics. They were uninterested, unmotivated, and he was growing increasingly frustrated.

While walking around the village one afternoon, he noticed a man following him. He had seen this man, always lurking around the school, watching him teach. A chill ran down Rajesh's spine. Who was this man? And why was he following him? The village was eerily quiet, with poor network, frequent power cuts and zero entertainment. His frustration deepened as he scrolled through Instagram, watching his friends back in Mumbai enjoying life at parties and get-togethers. "I thought this trip would be more exciting," he muttered.

When the weekend came, Rajesh visited his hometown and stayed over on Saturday and Sunday. His mother's joy at seeing him was palpable—tears of happiness streamed down her face as she pampered her son. Rajesh felt a renewed sense of happiness and peace, and this change of heart sparked an idea.

On Monday, he returned to the village and brought his phone to the classroom. He asked the kids to sing Bollywood songs with him, belting out tunes with exaggerated gestures and dance moves. But the kids stared wide-eyed as if he were a clown in a circus. He kept at it for several days, but nothing seemed to work.

Finally, he had had enough. He called his boss, his voice heavy with frustration. "Sir, I'm done here. Coming back to Mumbai." He packed his bags, feeling a deep sense of defeat. Here he was, someone who had always prided himself on never giving up, ready to quit after just a month.

As he sat in the jeep, waiting to leave the village for good, a wave of sadness washed over him. Had he given up so quickly? The jeep started moving, bumping along the uneven road, and as they passed by the village school, he heard something that made him sit up straight. The kids—those same kids who had seemed so uninterested — were singing. They were singing the tunes of the songs he had taught them! He couldn't make out the words, but the melody was unmistakable.

His heart skipped a beat. Was this real? Could this small sign be the breakthrough he had been waiting for? He glanced out the window, watching the children sing, and something shifted inside him in that moment.

The jeep kept moving, but Rajesh didn't. He made a decision. "Stop the car," he said. The driver looked puzzled but obeyed. Rajesh turned to him and said, "We're returning to the village."

And so, with renewed hope and determination, Rajesh did not just return back to the village, but also returned back to his inner light, ready to give it one more try.

Mindful Reflections: 》》

In a world that often glorifies success and winning, it's easy to lose sight of what truly matters. Life isn't defined by the accolades we accumulate or the milestones we check off. True fulfilment lies not in the excellence we achieve in material terms, but in the growth and transformation we experience along the way. Life is good when we focus on what to do, but it becomes truly excellent when we focus on who we become while doing it.

The true essence of life resides in the small, everyday moments that shape our journey. As the ancient Greek philosopher Seneca wisely put it, "Life is made of days." How we spend each day, the energy we bring to our routines, and the attention we give to each moment are the real indicators of a life well-lived. Each of us is a unique blend of traits, shaped by experiences that make us who we are. Though we may share commonalities with others through culture, family, or skills, each of us walks our own path, with our own purpose to discover.

Yet, this path isn't always easy. Life can be overwhelming, filled with moments of uncertainty and darkness. But even in those struggles, there's always a guiding light - hope. Hope isn't just an emotion - it's the beacon that keeps us moving forward when the way ahead is unclear. It's what helps us keep going, even in our darkest hours.

Often, sadness pulls us into the past, while anxiety drags us into the future. But peace is found in the present, in each breath, in the acknowledgment that we are alive right now. This awareness is transformative. It brings us back to the here and now, to the only place where we can truly live and act. Planning for the future is important, of course, and as humans, we're naturally driven by progression. But the best way to fuel our dreams and keep moving forward is by staying rooted in the present, grounded in the hope that tomorrow can be better than today.

As you walk through your own journey, remember that each day counts. Every breath, every step, and every small effort you make adds to the life you're building. It's not the trophies or titles that will define you long-term, but the consistency of your actions, the hope you carry, and the meaning you find in the everyday.

Breathe deeply and appreciate this right moment – You are Alive, and that is a gift. Every breath is a fresh start, a new opportunity to align with your purpose and live with intention. Embrace this truth, and live each day to your fullest potential.

"Happiness is not something ready-
made. It comes from your own actions."
- Dalai Lama

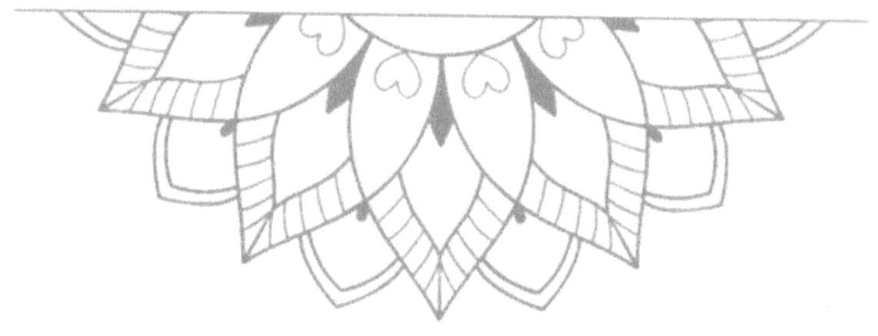

Become a ZERO and not a hero!

Once upon a time, a young boy named Hiroshi lived in a land where fierce warriors roamed. From a tender age, Hiroshi was captivated by the swift movements and unmatched skill of the samurais, who were revered as the greatest warriors of their time. The way they moved and the grace with which they wielded their swords was magical to the young boy. His father, noticing the spark in his son's eyes, decided to nurture his dream. He sent Hiroshi to train under a renowned master known for shaping boys into legends.

Hiroshi was a natural. He learned quickly, mastering the art of the sword with incredible speed. As he grew, so did his prowess, and it wasn't long before he became the most formidable warrior in the kingdom. His name struck fear into enemies' hearts, and his skill earned him admiration from all who witnessed his strength.

Despite his undeniable talent and the aura of invincibility that surrounded him, his guru often reminded him of a simple yet puzzling lesson: "Stay a warrior." Hiroshi couldn't understand why his guru would say this. After all, he was already celebrated as the greatest warrior of his time and his ambitions were set on achieving even greater feats.

Years passed and Hiroshi's legend only grew. He won countless battles for his kingdom, his reputation so fearsome that entire armies would surrender at the mere mention of his participation. In admiration of his unmatched skill, the king bestowed upon him the title of the GOAT - Greatest of All Time.

One evening, after returning victorious from another battle, the kingdom celebrated Hiroshi's success with grand festivities. His face was painted on walls, and his tales were carved into stone. Basking in the glory of his achievements, Hiroshi returned home, expecting nothing but peace. But as he entered his quarters, he noticed a tiny mouse sitting boldly on his bed.

Infuriated by what he saw as insulting his honour, Hiroshi drew his sword and chased the tiny intruder. The mouse darted under the bed and Hiroshi, with all his skill and strength, slashed at it furiously. But the mouse was quick, slipping through a small hole and disappearing.

Feeling both embarrassed and enraged, Hiroshi refused to let the mouse go. He overturned his entire house in search of it, slashing and stabbing at every sound, but the mouse remained elusive. Just as he was about to give up, he spotted the mouse again, perched mockingly on the edge of his sword. Hiroshi lunged at it in a rage, only to miss and slice his fingers instead. The pain was sharp, but what hurt more was his pride.

Consumed by fury, Hiroshi vowed to kill the mouse at any cost. He used every weapon in his arsenal, but the mouse seemed to be toying with him, always staying out of reach. By dawn, the once-mighty warrior was a wreck - exhausted, wounded and surrounded by the ruins of his home. His finger throbbed, and his ego was bruised beyond repair. In despair, he decided to seek counsel from his guru.

He ran to the mountain where his guru lived, arriving dishevelled and defeated. The guru, who had not seen his student in many years, was surprised to see him in such a state. Hiroshi poured out his frustrations, describing the nightmare of his encounter with the mouse. "I don't know what to do," he confessed. "I am the greatest warrior, yet this little mouse has made a fool of me. What will people think? My image is ruined."

The guru listened patiently, then smiled gently. "I think you need some rest," he said. "But first, let me give you someone who can help." The guru disappeared into his hut and returned moments later with a white-furred cat cradled in his arms.

Hiroshi was taken aback. Tears welled up in his eyes as he realised the solution's simplicity. As he held the cat, the guru's words echoed in his mind: "Remember what I taught you? Just stay a warrior."

At that moment, everything became clear. The lesson his guru had imparted all those years ago was not about fighting battles or seeking glory—it was about humility, wisdom, and knowing when to let go. Hiroshi finally understood that being a true warrior wasn't just about combat skills. It was about understanding his limits, embracing simplicity, and finding peace in knowing that sometimes, the smallest things can teach the greatest lessons.

(This story is inspired by an anonymous source. We do not claim any copyright or credits for it.)

Mindful Reflections: »

From a young age, we are taught specific values and beliefs that shape who we become. These guiding principles often go unquestioned, subtly steering our decisions and behaviours as we navigate life. But what if I told you that you can change these beliefs and values at any moment?

As humans, we carry the weight of numerous identities and labels – whether as sons, daughters, parents, spouses, or even bosses. We hold these roles with us, fulfilling our duties and responsibilities, and in the process, we often lose sight of who we are.

But what if, just for a moment, you could set down these layers? What if you could pause, release these identities and explore what it feels like to travel lightly, being simply you – not bound by the roles you play? I invite you to take that pause with me right now. Let go of the labels you've been carrying and reconnect with the essence of who you are beyond the expectations and responsibilities that define you.

You might discover a lighter, freer version of yourself, ready to embrace life with renewed clarity and purpose.

Often, these labels can blind us to our true potential, limiting our ability to see beyond the roles we've adopted. They can also lead to a judgmental view of ourselves, measuring our worth solely by how well we fulfil these roles.

Living a balanced life means embracing all the roles life requires of us without losing our true identity. It's about recognizing the values, interests, principles, and beliefs that guide you toward what genuinely matters. When you stay connected to your authentic self, you can face life's challenges with purpose, ensuring that each role you play enriches, rather than obscures, who you truly are.

To live freely, let go of the labels that confine you. Don't stay limited by past identities; set yourself free to embrace each day with your fullest potential. Think of it like a beloved sweater you've outgrown; it once fit perfectly but, over time, became too small. Eventually, you let it go, making space for something that better fits the person you've become. Embrace change and keep evolving toward your true self.

❖ ❖ ❖

"Your worst enemy cannot harm you as much as your own unguarded thoughts."
– Buddha

If you are egoistic then you are living in the past

It was a warm, bustling afternoon at Sage Vishvamitra's hermitage. The air was filled with the curiosity of eager young minds, gathered to learn from one of the greatest sages of their time. As Vishvamitra stood before his students, sharing his teachings on the nature of true wisdom, his mind began to wander back to a different time when he was not the sage they respected, but a powerful king, proud and unyielding.

As he spoke, a memory washed over him, vivid and consuming. He could almost feel the weight of the crown pressing against his brow, the richness of his royal robes flowing around him and the vastness of the kingdom he once commanded. Vishvamitra had ruled over a land of immense wealth and splendour, where every wish was granted with ease. His kingdom was a symbol of power, his reign marked by luxury and endless prosperity.

But in those moments of reflection, Vishvamitra understood something he hadn't back then. Despite all the power, wealth and admiration he had once held, his real journey had only begun in those days. As a king, he had been the epitome of command and control, admired by all. Yet, true wisdom - the kind that carves out destinies and shapes the soul - had eluded him, hidden beneath layers of pride and worldly success.

His voice softened as he continued, his students noticing the subtle change in his tone. "Today, before we delve into the heart of wisdom, I want to share a story with you," he began, pausing momentarily. "It is the tale of a proud king who learned, in the hardest way, what true wisdom is."

The students leaned in, captivated by this unexpected shift in the lesson. The once lively hermitage grew still, every ear tuned to the story that was about to unfold. Vishvamitra hesitated, not yet ready to reveal that the king in his tale was none other than himself. But his lessons were too valuable to keep hidden, especially from the eager young minds before him.

With quiet resolve, he began the story of his past, carefully unravelling the journey that had led him to the sagehood his students now revered. The transformation from king to sage, from pride to wisdom, was about to be told - but for now, it was simply the story of a king who had yet to understand what it meant to honestly know.

Vishvamitra began his story, his voice low but steady, the memory of the past unfolding like a distant echo. The students sat in silent anticipation, the hermitage filled with reverence.

"Once, a proud king driven by curiosity and ambition set out with his army," Vishvamitra said, his gaze distant, "to visit the great Sage Vashishta, a man known for his spiritual wisdom and peace."

He paused, letting the scene settle in his students' minds. "The king was welcomed like royalty. The hermitage, simple as it was, brimmed with warmth and hospitality. The sage greeted him humbly, yet with such respect that the king couldn't help but wonder how a mere hermit could afford such grandeur."

The students could almost feel the crisp breeze that had swept through the forest that day, the scent of burning incense lingering in the air and the murmur of life in the sage's hermitage. Vishvamitra continued, his voice rich with detail.

"As the king sat at the sage's table, marvelling at the feast laid before him, he finally asked, 'How is it, O Vashishta, that you, who live in such simplicity, can provide all of this? Where does this abundance come from?'"

Vishvamitra's tone shifted as he became the humble sage. "'It is not by my hand, great King,' Vashishta replied, calm and steady. 'I owe all this to Shabala, a holy cow providing everything needed. She is no ordinary creature, but one blessed by the divine.'"

Intrigued, Vishvamitra spoke again as the king. "'A cow? A treasure like that should be in the royal palace, where it can benefit an entire kingdom,'" he said, the king's voice growing sharper, more authoritative. "'Give her to me, Vashishta. She belongs with a king, not a hermit.'"

The students could hear the weight of the command, the unmistakable pride in the king's voice. Vishvamitra's face hardened as he slipped deeper into the role of his former self.

"But Vashishta only smiled," Vishvamitra continued, returning to the sage's calm demeanour. "'I cannot give her to you, great King,' he said gently. 'Shabala is part of this hermitage, and I am bound to her as she is to me. She will not leave.'"

A tense silence settled over the hermitage as Vishvamitra's voice darkened with the king's rising anger. "'You dare refuse a king?'" he growled, his fists tightening in frustration. "'I will not ask again, Vashishta. Give me the cow, or I will take her by force.'"

The students felt the tension building, their breaths caught in their chests. They could almost see the proud king's eyes burning with indignation, the fire of his ego flickering dangerously.

"But Vashishta did not flinch," Vishvamitra said quietly. "He stood firm, his calmness infuriating the king even more. With a final wave, the king ordered his soldiers to seize Shabala."

Vishvamitra's voice softened with emotion as he described the scene. "Shabala, poor Shabala, resisted. She fought against the soldiers, her eyes wide with fear and confusion. She cried out, tears streaming down her face as she struggled, unwilling to leave her home. Desperate, she broke free and ran to Vashishta, collapsing at his feet, her body trembling."

The students could feel the weight of her sorrow, the warmth of her breath and the soft rustling of her fur as she clung to the sage for protection.

"Help me, Master,' she pleaded, her voice quivering with fear. 'Why do they take me from you? Please, do not let them take me away!'"

Vishvamitra paused, his own heart heavy with the memory. "'Do not fear, Shabala,' Vashishta whispered as he knelt beside her, his hand resting on her head. 'No one will take you from me.'"

Vishvamitra continued his tale, his voice rich with emotion - "Moved by the sight of Shabala's tear-filled eyes and her desperate plea, Sage Vashishta knelt beside her, gently placing a comforting hand on her trembling form. His calm yet commanding voice echoed through the hermitage as he said, 'Summon your strength, Shabala. Defend yourself against those who seek to harm you.' With a sorrowful gaze, Shabala rose, her eyes glittering with divine power. At Vashishta's command, the air around her crackled with energy, and from the earth emerged a mighty army, solid and formidable. Their battle cry echoed across the hermitage as they charged the king's men.

The clash was swift and decisive. Though powerful, the king's forces did not match the conjured army. Dust filled the air, and the king's soldiers soon lay scattered and defeated. Furious and humiliated, the king bellowed, 'How dare you!' His face flushed with rage, and gripping his sword, he stormed into the battlefield, unwilling to accept such disgrace. 'A mere cow will not defeat me!'"

Vishvamitra's students listened intently, eager to hear what unfolded next. With a steady voice, the sage continued, "The king roared as he unleashed his might upon Shabala's magical army, his sword slicing through the air. But despite his strength, the army proved too powerful. One by one, his soldiers fell. Even his sons, who joined the battle, were reduced to ashes in a heartbeat. Panting and drenched in sweat, the king stood amidst the wreckage of his once-proud army, his heart pounding with rage but powerless to change his fate. Defeated and disgraced, he cast one final glance at Vashishta, his ego shattered."

Taking a deep breath, Vishvamitra added, "But that was not the end. Still consumed by pride, the king muttered through clenched teeth as he turned away, 'I will return.' He left his kingdom in the hands of his surviving son and retreated to the mountains, the sound of his footsteps heavy with defeat.

For years, he secluded himself in the frozen heights of the Himalayas. The biting cold pierced his skin, and hunger gnawed at him, but he endured, meditating day and night with unwavering focus, calling upon Lord Shiva. His body grew weak, but his resolve only strengthened. Finally, after relentless austerities, the sky above him crackled with divine light. Lord Shiva appeared before him, his voice thundering, 'You have proven your devotion, O king. I grant you celestial weapons. May they serve you well.'"

Vishvamitra's voice deepened as he recounted the king's return. "Armed with these divine gifts, the king returned to Vashishta's hermitage, his heart filled with pride and vengeance. 'This time,' he muttered, gripping the reins of his chariot, 'Vashishta will be nothing before my power.'

Without a word, he unleashed a fire weapon upon the hermitage. Flames roared and engulfed the once peaceful sanctuary, reducing it to ashes. But amid the smoke, Vashishta emerged, calm and unshaken, holding the brahmadanda, his holy staff.

'Your weapons cannot harm me, O king,' Vashishta said, his voice serene. The king hurled his celestial weapons - arrows of fire and lightning - but the power of Vashishta's staff effortlessly deflected each one. Growing more frustrated, the king unleashed his final weapon, the Brahmastra. Darkness enveloped the world as if the sun had been eclipsed. But once again, Vashishta's holy staff neutralised the attack. The darkness faded, and Vashishta stood untouched."

Vishvamitra paused, letting the weight of the story sink in. "The king collapsed to his knees, his chest heaving, his mind racing. But all his pride and rage had crumbled. In a whisper, he admitted, 'I have lost… not just this battle, but myself.'

Vashishta stepped forward, his eyes filled with understanding. 'True strength does not lie in weapons or power, O king,' he said softly. 'It lies in mastery over oneself and the wisdom to use one's strengths wisely.'

At that moment, the king realised the truth. His defeat was not in battle but in ego. He had been humbled, not by Vashishta's power, but by his ignorance. 'You are right,' the king acknowledged, bowing his head. 'I must rid myself of pride and all that binds me to this world.'

Vishvamitra concluded, 'And so, the king's command was met not by force, but by the quiet strength of Vashishta's love and the divine protection that Shabala deserved. A lesson that humbled the proud king, teaching him the true meaning of wisdom.'"

The hermitage was cloaked in heavy silence as Vishvamitra's story hung in the air. Each student was spellbound, anticipating more. As the session on true wisdom drew to a close, Vishvamitra quietly made his way to the centre of the hermitage, where the old, sprawling tree stood - where he often sought solace and reflection.

He lowered himself beneath its broad branches, the cool shade offering a moment of peace. As the gentle rustling of leaves whispered above him, he pondered the day's lesson. "Today," he thought, "I shared my story, but I could not reveal that it was my journey, filled with hard-earned lessons." He sighed softly, his gaze drifting to the tree's towering canopy. "Have I truly shed the layers of ego and pride?" he wondered. "Or is there still more within me to uncover before I can say I have fully grasped the essence of true wisdom?"

Sitting beneath the ancient tree, Vishvamitra realised that wisdom was not a destination but an ongoing path - one that required constant reflection, humility, and growth. Though he had come far, his journey was still unfolding.

(This story is inspired by the works of author Sunita Pant Bansal. We do not claim any copyright or credits for it.)

Mindful Reflections: 》》

Beneath the surface of pride and worldly success lies a simple truth – true wisdom can only be accessed once we let go of our ego. The ego is like a shadow that clouds our judgement, keeping us stuck in the past and preventing us from seeing our path forward. Whenever we allow it to take control, it drags us away from the present moment – the only place where happiness and peace exist.

Think about it. Every time your ego is triggered, it's usually rooted in something from your past. Whether it's a hurtful incident or an attachment to a label or identity, your ego pulls you backwards, leaving you dissatisfied. But isn't life about finding joy and contentment in this present moment? Yet, being a roller coaster ride of emotions every day!

This is why many of the world's greatest coaches and philanthropists encourage us to embrace a mindful lifestyle. Mindfulness allows you to accept yourself as you are right now without clinging to the past or projecting into the future. It's a powerful practice that pulls you back to the present, offering a sense of peace and clarity that can help you make better decisions for a better future – free from the grip of ego.

The ego is essential to our emotional landscape, driving our need for validation and superiority based on past achievements and identities. While it's a natural aspect of self-preservation, an unchecked ego can distort reality, making us overly attached to the past and leading to harmful actions today.

Think of ego as a mental reflex, like hunger or fear. It influences how we see and react to the world, often pulling us away from the present moment. By becoming aware of our ego, we can prevent it from controlling our actions. This awareness helps us make clearer, more mindful choices, fostering true contentment to find peace and happiness.

When ego blinds you, it often leads to actions that can harm you and those closest to you. Awareness is key. By recognising when your ego is at play, you can avoid the pitfalls of pride and instead focus on what matters - living in harmony with yourself and your loved ones.

I invite you to take a few minutes to reflect on a recent situation where you felt irritated, hurt or overly proud. Journaling has often helped millions of successful people accept themselves and access their true potential from deep within. If you could, write down how this emotion linked back to a past incident, a label, or an identity you were holding onto. Now, let's consider how things might have been different if you had been fully present and focused on what was happening rather than reacting from a place of ego. Take a few more minutes and self-reflect; take all the time you need here.

Next time you feel your ego being triggered, pause, take a deep breath, and remind yourself - I am more than my past or my labels. I am here, now, at this moment. I genuinely persuade you to participate in this simple exercise that can help you begin to recognize when your ego is taking control. It will allow you to be aware of it and then just let it go, returning to the present, where true peace resides.

"In a conflict between the heart and
the brain, follow your heart."
- Swami Vivekananda

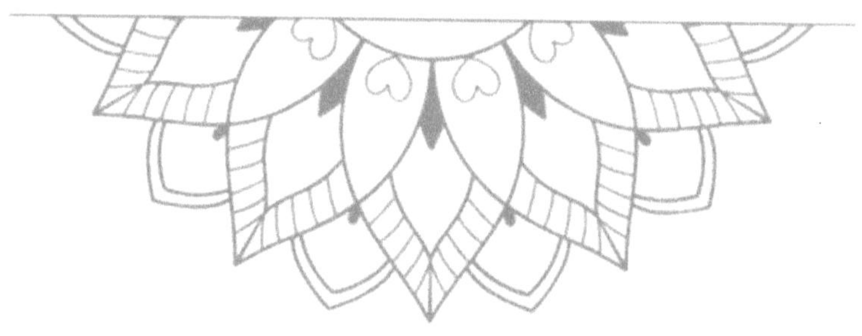

The story of Akbar and Tansen

In the heart of ancient India, Emperor Akbar was celebrated for his wisdom and strength and his exceptional court, filled with rare talents. Among them was Tansen, a virtuoso whose voice was so enchanting that it could transcend the ordinary bounds of music and transport listeners to ethereal realms. Tansen's presence in Akbar's darbar was a source of immense pride, a jewel among many in the emperor's court.

One evening, as various kings from neighbouring kingdoms gathered at Akbar's palace, the emperor summoned Tansen with a special request. "Tonight," Akbar announced, "you must present the finest performance ever witnessed in my court. It must be something truly rare and extraordinary."

Tansen, ever the proficient artist, accepted the challenge with grace. The darbar hall was abuzz with anticipation as the evening unfolded. As Tansen took his place, he addressed the audience, "Tonight, I will present a composition created by my revered guru. This piece has never been heard before."

With Akbar's kingly nod of approval, Tansen began his performance. The hall fell into an utter silence so profound that it seemed to hold its breath. Tansen's rich and divine voice wove through the air like a golden thread, delivering a piece of such exquisite beauty that it left the entire assembly spellbound. When he concluded, the silence persisted as if the darbar was still absorbed in the magic of his song. Only after a few moments did the audience begin to stir, their stunned admiration transforming into zealous applause. Kings threw gold and diamonds in tribute, and Tansen graciously accepted their awards.

As night fell and Akbar wandered through his private gardens, he reflected on Tansen's extraordinary performance. It was as if Tansen's performance had a piece of his heart forever. The music had left him exhilarated, an emotion that lingered long after the echoes of Tansen's voice had faded. A thought sprouted in King Akbar's mind that led him to summon Tansen for an urgent meeting.

When Tansen arrived, he found the emperor waiting with a gleam of curiosity in his eyes. "Tansen," Akbar said warmly, "your performance tonight was miraculous. I am deeply grateful for the gift you've shared with us."

"It was my honour, my lord," Tansen replied with a humble bow.

Akbar's eyes twinkled with eagerness. "Since this composition is from your guru, he must also be an extraordinary musician. I would very much like to hear him sing. Could you bring him to the darbar?"

Tansen's expression grew dingy. "With all due respect, my lord, my guru will not come to the darbar."

"Why not?" Akbar asked, puzzled and offended. "Is he too proud to visit the court of the emperor?"

"Not at all," Tansen explained. "But my guru sings only for the divine, not any human audience. If you wish to hear him, we must travel to him."

Akbar, though intrigued and somewhat taken aback, agreed to accompany Tansen. The following morning, they embarked on a journey through deserts and dense forests to the remote abode of Tansen's guru.

After two days of back-breaking travel, they arrived at a humble hut deep in the forest. Tired yet eager, Akbar followed Tansen, who requested that the guards remain at a distance. As they approached the modest dwelling, Tansen instructed, "We must stay here and wait. My guru will come out soon."

A figure emerged from the hut, an old sage with a serene appearance and a long beard that spoke of years of solitude. Eager to meet the great musician, Akbar stepped forward, but Tansen restrained him. "We cannot approach him. My guru sings solely for the divine."

Baffled but patient, Akbar listened intently as a soft, melodious voice began to fill the air. The music, imbued with a sacred quality, transcended earthly concerns. Tansen whispered, "He is singing the Malhar, raga of rain."

As the notes danced through the forest, a miraculous phenomenon occurred. Thunder rumbled, and the heavens opened up, releasing a gentle rain. Akbar and Tansen stood in awe, overwhelmed by the divine experience of witnessing such profound dedication to music.

Akbar turned to Tansen with newfound understanding on their way back to the palace. "I now see why you spoke of your guru's singing as divine. He does not seek an audience or accolades; his music is an offering to the gods."

Tansen nodded, his heart brimming with pride and respect for his guru. The emperor had witnessed something extraordinary - a testament to the purity of artistry and devotion that rises above human accolades and finds its true expression in the divine.

As they continued their journey back, Akbar, still absorbed in the wonder of the experience, turned to Tansen with a thoughtful expression. "Have you ever considered following your guru's path? To sing solely for the divine, as he does? Would you ever leave my court to find peace in such a remote place?"

Akbar's voice carried a hint of concern, worried about losing such a virtuoso from his darbar. Understanding the emperor's apprehension, Tansen responded with calm assurance. "My dear emperor, I deeply respect my guru and his way of life, but I am exactly where I wish to be. I find my purpose and fulfilment in serving your court, where my music can touch many lives. I am grateful for the honour and opportunities you have given me, and I am content in this role."

With a respectful bow, Tansen expressed his gratitude to Akbar. The emperor, reassured and appreciative of Tansen's dedication, smiled warmly. The bond between them was strengthened, grounded in mutual respect and the shared understanding of the unique paths Tansen and his guru walked - one in the divine silence of the forest, the other amidst the vibrant life of the court.

(This story is inspired by an anonymous source. We do not claim any copyright or credits for it.)

Mindful Reflections: 》

In the desperate pursuit for a purposeful life, many of us struggle with choosing between two distinct paths - one marked by personal recognition and influence and the other characterised by spiritual devotion and solitude. This contrast often prompts deep introspection about how best to serve the world and align our lives with our true purpose.

On one hand, there is the allure of making a significant impact in the public sphere. This path offers the potential for recognition, achievement and the opportunity to influence others on a large scale. It can be immensely rewarding, as it allows us to use our talents and skills to make a visible difference in the world.

On the other hand, there is the path of inner peace and spiritual dedication. This route involves a deep connection with one's values and purpose, often leading to a more introspective and solitary existence. It may not offer the same public acclaim, but it provides profound satisfaction derived from living in harmony with one's principles and serving a higher cause, fulfilling our reason to exist.

Choosing between these paths can be challenging. Sometimes, discovering our purpose is only the beginning. The real struggle lies in determining how to fulfil this purpose in a way that aligns with our values and meets the world's expectations.

The journey to finding and living out your purpose can be complex, especially when faced with the choice between public influence and personal fulfilment. By reflecting on your values, visualising your ideal life and setting intentional goals, you can navigate this journey with greater clarity and conviction. Ultimately, the path you choose should resonate with your true self and provide a sense of fulfilment that goes beyond external recognition.

To find your path and gain clarity, let's engage ourselves in the following exercise:

1. Define Your Values – Identify your core values, interests or principles that guide your life. Understanding what is most important to you is the foundation for making meaningful and long-lasting decisions.

2. Assess Your Current Path – Evaluate how well your current life aligns with these values. Are you following a path that reflects your deepest beliefs and desires or are you simply conforming to external pressures and expectations?

3. Consider Different Paths – Reflect on two potential paths: one focused on public impact and recognition and the other centred on personal fulfilment and spiritual connection. Which aspects of each resonate with you? How do these aspects align with your identified values?

4. Visualise Your Ideal Life – Imagine a day in your ideal life. What activities are you engaged in? Who are you

with? How do you feel? Assess how this vision aligns with your values and purpose.

5. Set Intentional Goals – Based on your reflections, set specific, actionable goals to move closer to your ideal life. These goals might include pursuing new opportunities, adjusting your current path or incorporating practices that align with your values.

6. Journal Your Insights – Document your thoughts and insights from this exercise. Regular journaling can help you stay connected with your purpose and track your progress, ensuring that you remain focused on living a life true to your values amidst the distractions of everyday life.

❖ ❖ ❖

"Peace comes from within. Do not seek it without." - Buddha

Watch your THOUGHTS as they become your DESTINY

Baman's bungalow stood in profound solitude, its once pristine white walls now dulled by years of neglect. The house's grandeur, with its elegant pillars and fancy balcony, seemed like a historical object from a bygone era, struggling to remain distinguished against the encroaching wilderness of the overgrown garden. Here, wild ivy snaked its way up the façade, twisting and turning with a strong grip, while untidy shrubs and tangled vines masked the once neatly trimmed hedges.

Since his wife's passing and his children's move abroad, Baman had lived alone, his only company the echoes of his once thriving business and the persistent ticking of the grandfather clock in his study - a rhythmic reminder of time slipping by. The once-vibrant life of Baman's home had faded into a quiet emptiness, punctuated only by the occasional creak of floorboards or the gentle drift of dust particles caught in the sunlight streaming through cobweb-covered windows.

The air was thick with the remains of a bustling past, where laughter and conversation had once filled the spaces now deprived of life. The walls, adorned with faded photographs and mementoes, told stories of when Baman's life had been rich with social connections and familial warmth. Those memories seemed like distant echoes, swallowed by the vast, empty rooms.

Friends had long since drifted away, unable to penetrate the walls Baman had fortified around himself. Once frequent visitors, relatives had become shadows of the past, their visits dwindling into mere memories of a time when Baman's aloof look had not yet estranged him from their lives. The weight of isolation pressed heavily on the bungalow, its stillness a testament to the solitude that had become Baman's constant companion.

One crisp autumn afternoon, Baman wandered through his garden, his steps muted by the rustling of fallen leaves. He paused by the rare flowering hedge, where a delicate white-furred cat walked among the plants. With eyes like polished amber, the cat seemed to regard him with an unspoken understanding.

"Hello there," Baman murmured, kneeling, his old bones creaking in protest. He reached out a hand, his fingers brushing the cat's soft fur. The cat inched closer, brushing its body against Baman's legs with an affectionate purr. A warmth spread through Baman's chest - a rare sensation of being needed.

From that day, the cat became his constant companion.

Every morning, Baman would set a small plate of milk by the open window. The cat, like clockwork, would slip in through the gap in the grill door, its presence filling the silent house. They spent afternoons sprawled together on the big brown sofa, Baman's old radio softly playing RD Burman's melodies, the tunes weaving a magic that seemed to captivate them both.

Baman would settle into his favourite armchair, the cat curling beside him on the big brown sofa. As the television flickered with the latest reality show, Baman would turn to his feline companion with a grin.

"Can you believe this?" he'd say, gesturing towards the screen. "They're all pretending to be friends, but you can see right through them. It's all about the drama."

The cat, its golden eyes fixed on the TV, nodded slightly, its head bobbing in rhythm with Baman's enthusiastic gestures.

"Oh, look at that," Baman would continue, pointing at a particularly outrageous scene. "She's claiming she didn't know about the surprise party, but she was caught on camera talking about it! Can you imagine? The nerve!"

The cat responded with a soft purr, as if in agreement, and Baman chuckled, his laughter mingling with the low hum of the television.

"You're right," Baman would say, scratching the cat behind the ears. "These reality shows are just a big performance. But it's fun to watch them stumble over their lies."

In these shared moments, the world outside seemed to

vanish. The comfort of the cat's presence made Baman forget the loneliness that usually surrounded him. They were partners in this small, private escape, where the outside world's noise faded into the background, leaving only the warmth of their companionship.

But one Saturday morning, Baman's routine was disrupted. He sipped his tea, savouring the crispness of the newspaper column he adored and glanced at the clock. By mid-morning, the cat had not appeared. Baman's anticipation turned into anxiety. He waited in his armchair, the shadows lengthening as the hours passed, but the cat was nowhere to be seen.

By afternoon, Baman's unease had escalated into worry. He kept doors and windows open, hoping to glimpse his companion. As evening approached, the silence of the house grew oppressive. The phone calls from his children went unanswered, Baman's mind was consumed with thoughts of his missing friend.

Night fell, and with it came a thunderstorm. The rain lashed against the windows, and the wind howled like a mournful wail. Baman hurried around the house, closing the windows. As he reached the one facing the garden, lightning illuminated something strange in the downpour. He grabbed a flashlight and peered outside.

The sight was shocking. There, drenched and lifeless, was the cat - its body awkwardly stretched, one leg reaching skyward. Baman's breath caught in his throat. The torch nearly slipped from his trembling hands as he stumbled back inside, tears streaming down his face. The heartache was overwhelming, his chest tightening with each beat.

His world seemed to unravel, the one source of solace he'd found now taken from him.

Desperate, he picked up the phone and dialled Pratap, an old friend from the municipal corporation. His voice cracked with despair.

"Hello… hello, Pratap? I'm so sorry to call you at this hour, but… something has happened. Ma ma my cat… There is this cat and it's dead in my garden. It's getting soaked in this rain and I don't know what to do. I need someone to come and take care of it. Tomorrow? No, tomorrow's too late. Please, first thing in the morning."

Baman couldn't sleep that night. The relentless rain pounded against the windows, and the sight of the cat's lifeless form haunted him. The following day, the cat's body looked even more dismal - flies swarmed, and the stench was unbearable. Crows circled, pecking at the remains, a macabre scene that Baman could hardly bear.

He called Pratap again, his voice rising in frustration. "Pratap, what's going on? I was told someone would come today. The cat is still here, and nobody has shown up. Are you telling me someone came and saw nothing? I'm not making this up! If you don't send someone now, I'll have to handle this myself."

The phone call ended in a desperate slam. Baman's anger and confusion spiralled into a grim realisation that maybe, just maybe, they had failed him on purpose. Pratap, growing concerned about his friend's odd behaviour, decided to visit Baman himself. The rain had finally stopped and as he approached Baman's bungalow, he saw a chilling sight in the garden. The body of the cat was gone.

Instead, there was Baman, lifeless and sprawled in a disturbing pose - one leg outstretched toward the sky, his body dismantled in the same way as the cat's had been.

Pratap's heart raced as he rushed to Baman's side, his face pale with shock. The truth was undeniable - Baman's grief and isolation had driven him to this tragic end. The realisation struck Pratap like a thunderbolt, leaving him to wrestle with honouring his old friend's last moments.

(This story is inspired by the works of author Ratnakar Matkari. We do not claim any copyright or credits for it.)

Mindful Reflections: ⟩⟩

Dreams can indeed come true, but they require more than just wishing; they demand the right mindset and a positive thought process. The thoughts you nurture each day deeply influence your actions, and those actions, in turn, shape your destiny. To achieve your dreams, it's essential to keep them at the forefront of your mind. This isn't about daydreaming but rather consciously focusing on your goals. For instance, if your dream is to become a successful entrepreneur, regularly envisioning this success can inspire you to take the necessary steps to turn it into reality. Positive thinking acts as a magnet, attracting opportunities and giving you the strength to overcome obstacles. Conversely, negative thoughts can hinder progress. Constant doubts and fears lead to procrastination or self-sabotage, preventing forward movement.

Mahatma Gandhi's words offer profound insight: "Watch your thoughts, for they will become your words; watch your words, for they will become your actions; watch your actions, for they will become your habits; watch your habits, for they will forge your values; and watch your values, for they will shape your destiny." All our negative thoughts, if left unchecked, can turn into destructive actions, forming habits that lead to an unwanted and fearful future.

As this realisation of dreams requires more than mere envisioning; it requires deliberate focus on positive thinking, resilience, and mindful action. Your thoughts influence your actions, which shape your habits and ultimately, your destiny. By fostering a positive mindset and managing negative thoughts, you can confidently advance toward your dreams. As Gandhiji's wisdom suggests, the journey from thoughts to destiny is a continuous cycle – what you think today shapes your future. Embrace your dreams with positivity and watch them unfold into reality.

Practising self-awareness ensures that your thoughts work in your favour. A simple habit of mindful living allows you to identify negative thoughts without judgement and accept them without resistance. Once you recognize these negative thoughts, could you imagine replacing them with positive affirmations aligned with your potential? Surround yourself with positivity by engaging with supportive people, carefully curating the content you consume, and practising gratitude. This shift can lead to profound changes in your mindset.

Visualisation is another powerful tool for reinforcing commitment. Spending time each day imagining your dreams as if they've already been achieved makes them feel more real, motivating you to align your actions with your goals. Break down your dreams into small, actionable steps and celebrate each small victory to maintain positivity and momentum.

Self-belief is fundamental in this process. Confidence in your abilities fuels persistence and helps you navigate uncertainty. When you believe in your dreams, you send a powerful message to yourself and the universe, increasing the likelihood of success. The power of belief cannot be underestimated on the journey to making dreams a reality.

Maintaining a positive mindset benefits not only you but also those around you. You radiate an inspiring aura. Your enthusiasm and determination create a ripple effect, motivating others to pursue their dreams and fostering a supportive environment where everyone can thrive.

As you finish reading this, take a moment to reflect on your own dreams. Grab a notepad or your journal, and write down one immediate dream you wish to realise. Be as detailed as possible. Imagine yourself living that dream – what year is it? Who is with you? What are you wearing as this dream is now your reality? Where are you, and what time of day or night is it? Let your imagination flow freely and capture every detail you see, feel, and experience in this moment of your dream becoming reality.

"Rather than walking on the treadmill of life unconsciously, mindfulness puts you in control." - Ellen Langer

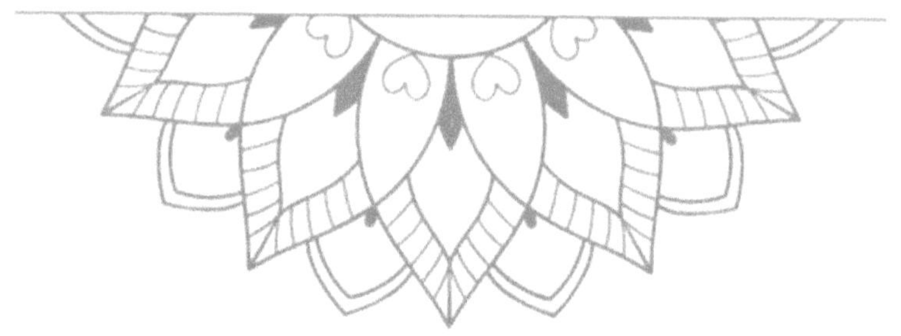

Do you believe in SACRIFICE?

While I was at an event called 'Rare Station', a unique gathering where anyone from around the world could share their story, I felt a mix of excitement and curiosity. The atmosphere was charged with anticipation, with people eager to either inspire or unburden themselves. Whether it was a tale of triumph or a heavy confession, this was an open mic for the soul. I had signed up to share my own story, a real-life account of how small investments had led to unexpectedly huge profits.

As I stepped up to the mic, the spotlight felt warmth on my face, the murmur of the crowd fading into a respectful hush. I took a breath and launched into my tale. Seven minutes later, the room erupted in applause. I could hear scattered voices calling out, "Well done!" and "Incredible story!" The buzz of appreciation filled me with a quiet sense of accomplishment. It wasn't just the applause that pleased me; it was in a space where stories could breathe, where I could talk about something I rarely discussed finance and where I could also listen.

For me, Rare Station wasn't just an opportunity to share. It was a break from my routine, a chance to delve into the minds of others. As a coach, I'm always curious about what holds people back from reaching their full potential but also what drives them to succeed. There's magic in that balance, and I was eager to hear more stories.

One story stuck with me. A businessman stood confidently at the mic, peddling his "special chocolates" designed to solve all women's problems. I couldn't help but smirk at his overblown claims. "Chocolates to fix womanhood," I muttered under my breath, shaking my head. His overconfidence was amusing, to say the least, and I caught myself giggling at his audacity.

The audience was still abuzz from the last speaker, sharing amused glances, when the host stepped onto the stage. "Our next speaker," she announced, "will be our final one for today. Please, no recordings or photographs." The unexpected request immediately grabbed everyone's attention. In a space filled with storytellers eager for recognition, it was puzzling to hear someone decline the opportunity for visibility. Personally, I had hoped snippets of my own story might find their way onto social media, maybe even spark a few conversations.

As I pondered this, a woman walked onto the stage. She was dressed in a traditional salwar kurta, her head and face completely covered by her dupatta, and only her eyes were visible. They were dark, intense, and seemed to carry both fear and defiance. The room fell into a hushed silence.

"Please," she repeated, her voice soft yet unwavering, "no videos or pictures."

With that, she gently pulled the dupatta down, revealing her face and letting it rest on her shoulders. Though the action was simple, it felt profoundly significant, like the unveiling of a secret that had been long hidden. Now, with her entire face visible, her eyes held the full attention of the room. The mood shifted. What had been a lively, casual atmosphere moments earlier turned solemn, as if everyone was bracing for what was about to be revealed.

Then, she began to speak. Her voice, steady but laden with emotion, carried the weight of something deeply personal, something that demanded not just to be heard but felt. I straightened in my seat, drawn in by her quiet strength.

The dimly lit room hummed with anticipation as she approached the microphone. Her face, pale but resolute, reflected the gravity of her story. She hesitated briefly, her fingers trembling slightly as she gripped the podium space. After a deep breath, she began, "Hi everyone. Today, I'm sharing a story I've never told anyone. Honestly, I've been too afraid. Telling it might mean risking my life."

The silence in the room was palpable, heavy with curiosity and concern. All eyes were fixed on her as the intensity of her words settled over us like a blanket. I leaned forward in my seat, my heart racing, sensing that we were about to witness something deeply personal and vulnerable.

"I was born in a small village between Hyderabad and Karnataka," she continued, her voice steady but low. "In my family, having children wasn't about love, but about fulfilling a duty. I'm the eldest, with a younger sister and a brother. My parents always treated my brother as the crown jewel, the future 'man of the house,' as if his gender made him more valuable. From a young age, I knew my worth in their eyes was less, simply because I was a girl."

Her words painted vivid pictures of her life, a dusty village where tradition ruled, where boys were groomed for leadership and girls for slavery. I could feel the weight of centuries-old beliefs pressing down on her, as if an invisible chain shackled her. The air felt thick with unspoken pain as she spoke.

"I had to beg, plead with my parents just to let me study," she said, a bitter smile tugging at the corners of her lips. "When they finally let me finish my graduation, I thought I'd won a battle. But it was only the beginning. Like every other girl in my village, the moment I graduated, my parents found me a husband. They didn't care about his education; he had only studied till the 10th grade or who he was as a person. For them, marriage was the next 'duty.'"

There was a brief pause, the kind that made you realise how quiet everything had become. Even the distant traffic outside seemed muted. When she continued, her voice was softer but no less powerful.

"I didn't know this man before I married him. We weren't allowed to speak, let alone spend any time alone before the wedding. But I told myself I could adjust. After all, isn't that what women are told? To adjust, to accept? Little did I know that my life was about to become a nightmare. He was rude and disrespectful. I felt like a servant in his house, not a wife. My mother-in-law remained silent as if this was normal. And maybe, in her world, it was."

I could see her hands clutching the edges of the podium tightly as if anchoring herself in the moment. She took a deep breath before continuing.

"I had two sons with him, and I decided to make them my purpose. If nothing else, I would raise them well. But my husband's abuse only worsened. He began hitting me for anything and everything. I confided in my parents once, hoping for some kind of support. But my mother just said, 'This is your family now. You have to find your own way.'"

The room was deathly still. Her voice, though calm, held years of unshed tears, bottled rage, and a bone-deep weariness.

"I couldn't take it anymore. I thought about running away. I even told my sons we would escape together, but my younger son told the family. That night, I was locked in a dark room. They were punishing me for even thinking about freedom."

A murmur of disbelief rippled through the audience. The woman continued, her voice tightening with the memory.

"I thought I would die there. But then I saw a small, jammed window. With all the strength I had left, I pried it open using a rod. Dust and dirt flew into my face, but that moment felt like a glimpse of hope. I squeezed my body through that window and ran. I ran until my legs couldn't carry me anymore, and when I stopped, I realised I didn't even know where I was. But I was free. For the first time in years, I was free."

The emotional strain in the room was nearly unbearable. I found myself gripping my seat, wondering how this story would end. She wiped her eyes with the edge of her dupatta and continued.

"I ended up in Pune. The city felt huge and daunting, but it also felt like a fresh start. I found a job as a teacher, and for the first time, I was able to live the life I'd always dreamed of, independent and educated. I even started pursuing my master's degree in teaching. But the ache never leaves me. It's been five years since I saw my sons. I see their pictures on Facebook sometimes, and it hurts to know I'm missing their childhoods. My husband still sends me threats, promising to kill me if I ever return."

She paused, her eyes scanning the room, filled with strangers who now knew her most intimate pain.

"I live every day looking over my shoulder, afraid that he'll find me. But today, telling you all my story, I feel lighter, like a part of that burden has been lifted. Maybe one day, I'll reunite with my children. Maybe one day, I'll be free of this fear."-

She paused again, her eyes glistening, then spoke softly, "I haven't told you my name until now. But I think it's time. My name is Smita. And this is my story."

The room erupted in applause, but it wasn't the loud, celebratory kind. It was a slow, emotional acknowledgement of her strength and resilience. Smita stood there, still and strong, her journey far from over, but her voice was finally heard.

At that moment, her story wasn't just hers anymore. It belonged to all of us.

Mindful Reflections: »

Life doesn't always feel fair, does it? We often find ourselves travelling through challenges, disappointments, and unmet expectations. Yet, in the midst of all this, life has a way of offering us gifts we never asked for, surprises that enrich our journey in ways we couldn't have imagined. While we may not receive everything we seek, life often compensates us in unexpected and beautiful ways.

You've probably heard the saying, "To gain something, you must lose something." But is that really true? When we think deeply, it becomes a more nuanced question. Some may say yes, agreeing that sacrifices are necessary for growth and achievement. But pause for a moment; what exactly have you sacrificed? Was it time, a passion, or perhaps a dream you placed on hold for other priorities? And more importantly, do you still wish for those things today?

The truth is that life is full of choices, and sometimes, we give up one thing to make room for something we feel is more important at that moment. But as time goes on, we might find ourselves wondering if it's time to bring those sidelined ambitions back into focus. Could it be that the sacrifices we thought were permanent are actually just pauses on a longer journey?

It's easy to feel like the scapegoat - the one sacrificed for others in these moments. But what if I told you that you don't always have to make those hard sacrifices? The universe, or whatever higher force you believe in, often provides exactly what we need, even when it doesn't align perfectly with our desires. The key is in being mindful - truly aware of the blessings we have, and open to receiving what we might not even realise we're asking for.

Take a moment to reflect on your journey. Are there dreams you've put aside? Have sacrifices left you feeling incomplete? If so, it's time to shed light on those forgotten ambitions. Life has a way of granting second chances, offering us new perspectives, and surprising us when we least expect it.

In the end, you don't have to be the scapegoat. But when you're constantly prioritising others, where do you place yourself? At the very end or near the top? Because if you put yourself last, you're setting the tone for others to treat you the same way. Fill yourself up before giving to the world. Trust the process, stay mindful, and keep your heart open to life's unexpected gifts. Sometimes, what you lose is an open space for what you're about to gain.

"Breathe. Let go. And remind yourself that
this very moment is the only one you know
you have for sure." - Oprah Winfrey

Humans progress only in the presence of a SHARK

It was just another Monday morning. Kenji, still muzzy from sleep, sat up in bed, rubbing his eyes as the soft light filtered through the blinds. His mind was already running through his mental to-do list, meetings, numbers, strategies - but before he could get far, his phone rang.

The familiar name flashed across the screen: Akira. His business partner, always the early bird, was calling far earlier than usual.

Kenji answered with a yawn, "Morning, Akira. What's up?"

On the other end of the line, Akira's voice buzzed with excitement, brimming with energy. "Kenji! Have you seen today's newspaper?" he practically shouted, unable to contain his joy.

Kenji blinked, confused. "What? No, not yet…"

Akira buzzed again, "Check it! Now! You won't believe it!"

Intrigued, Kenji climbed out of bed and walked toward his front door, where the daily newspaper had been slipped under the frame. He picked it up while rubbing his groggy eyes to generate some vision to read.

The bold headline on the front page caught his eye immediately. His heart skipped a beat. There it was - a picture of him and Akira standing side by side, both smiling widely, with their names bold in the headline: "Fishing Pioneers Turn Dream into Reality - The Millionaires Who Defied the Odds!"

Kenji's breath caught in his throat as his eyes scanned the article, detailing their journey from struggling fishermen to business magnates. The tale of their success was splashed across the front page of one of Japan's leading newspapers, complete with their story of innovation, perseverance and victory.

He couldn't help but grin as he held the paper up to the light. "We did it," he whispered to himself. Bringing the phone back to his ear, he finally responded to Akira, his voice filled with awe. "We did it, dear partner. We really did it."

Akira laughed, his voice full of pride and relief. "I told you this day would come, didn't I? The whole country's talking about us!"

Kenji sank into his couch, still clutching the newspaper, his mind racing back to the struggles, the endless nights of brainstorming and the risks they'd taken. From installing freezers to finally getting it right, it had been a rollercoaster. But they had done it. They had turned their impossible dream into a reality.

"Our story… it's everywhere," Akira continued, his voice softer now. "We're the ones who made the impossible possible."

Kenji closed his eyes, letting the words settle in. Their success was not just about the money - it was about the journey. The risks they had taken, the setbacks they had faced and the resilience that carried them through adversity.

"Akira," he said, his voice thick with emotion, "this is only the beginning."

With a contented sigh, Kenji ended the call, knowing they would meet soon at the office to celebrate.

Standing on his apartment balcony, Kenji gazed at the bustling city below. The crisp morning air carried the faint scent of the sea, instantly transporting him back to where it all began. Today was a day of triumph - their latest contract had solidified their place as Japan's top seafood distributor. Yet, as the golden light of dawn bathed the skyline, Kenji's mind drifted to a time when success seemed as elusive as the fresh fish they had once struggled to deliver.

He could still see it clearly - the tranquil fishing village by the sea, where life revolved around the ocean's bounty. Back then, the waters teemed with fish and the villagers thrived on their daily, abundant catch. But with time, those vibrant shoals had reduced. The once-full nets came back nearly empty, and the villagers' eager anticipation for their evening feasts turned to frustration and despair.

Kenji, back then, was just a young fisherman, and he had hope running in his veins and determination in his heart. Where others saw hopelessness in the ocean's barren depths, Kenji saw a challenge. He wasn't ready to surrender. He remembered that day vividly, the wind howling around him, his hands gripping the wheel of his boat with white-knuckled resolve as he decided to venture farther than any fisherman before him.

The sea had stretched endlessly before him, and each day brought uncertainty. Yet Kenji pressed on, pushing his boat into uncharted waters, praying the ocean would yield its hidden treasures.

It had, but not as expected. When he returned with nets overflowing, the villagers gathered at the docks, their faces alight with hope. But the joy was temporary. The fish, though abundant, had lost their flavour. They had been out of the water too long, and the villagers' excitement faded. Kenji's heart sank as disappointment washed over him. The dream of reviving the village fishery slipped further from his grasp.

That's when Akira burst into the picture, his fiery ambition lighting up the dark cloud of doubt hanging over them. Kenji smiled at the memory of his friend's excitement, the way his eyes gleamed with a new idea.

"Why not install freezers on the boats?" Akira had proposed one evening, his voice brimming with confidence. "We'll catch the fish, freeze them immediately at sea and preserve the freshness. It's bold, it's innovative, and it's exactly what we need."

Kenji was lured by this idea, and Akira's enthusiasm was

infectious. It was their best shot. They knew it wouldn't be easy—it would take significant investment from their already sinking savings—but they had a business mindset and a drive to succeed.

"We'll make it work," Kenji had said, more to convince himself than to Akira.

So, they had set sail once again, this time with high hopes and cutting-edge technology, believing their investment would finally turn their fortunes around.

But fate, as it often does, had other plans. The Japanese palate, so refined and selective, immediately noticed the difference between fresh and frozen fish. Their grand plan had collapsed. The freezers they had invested in so heavily now felt like a sinking stone, dragging their dreams down with it. Kenji could still remember the bitter disappointment, the way their hopes had faded - along with their self-belief.

Kenji leaned against the balcony railing, recalling just how close they had come to giving up. The success they were celebrating today wouldn't have existed if, after their second failure, they hadn't decided to visit the city's public library for business lessons. Of course, it hadn't been Kenji's idea. He had never been one for books, preferring the salt air and open sea to the quiet of a library. But Akira, always the one with an unquenchable curiosity for new ideas, had insisted.

"Come on, Kenji," Akira had said, his eyes bright with determination. "We're missing something. Let's hit the library. There's bound to be something we can learn from other businesses."

Kenji sighed, already weary from their latest setback. "The library? You think a book is going to solve our fish problem?" he had asked, raising an eyebrow.

Akira had grinned. "Well, it can't hurt, right? At least we'll be doing something."

And so, reluctantly, Kenji followed Akira into the city's public library. They had wandered the aisles, with Kenji dragging his feet while Akira eagerly flipped through pages. Kenji had slumped in a chair, watching his friend dart from shelf to shelf.

"Have you found something yet, genius?" Kenji asked after a while, his voice laced with scepticism.

"Patience, Kenji, patience," Akira had replied, still scanning the shelves. Then, after a few moments of silence, he had stopped, a triumphant gleam in his eyes. "Here it is. Listen to this - 'Man thrives oddly enough only in the presence of a challenging environment.'"

Kenji had stared at him, unimpressed. "And what's that supposed to mean?"

Akira had grinned and sat down across from him, the excitement in his voice contagious. "It means we've been looking at this all wrong! The problem isn't just about catching the fish, it's about keeping them fresh. We need to create an environment that forces them to stay alive and active until we're back on shore."

Kenji had frowned, confused. "How do you plan to do that?"

"Sharks!" Akira had said, his grin widening. "We put

small sharks in the tanks with the fish. The fish will be so busy trying to survive, they'll stay lively and fresh."

Kenji, not sure how useful this idea was, shaking his head, said, "Sharks? I don't know, Akira."

But even as he was unable to think straight, still hampered by their last failure, a small part of him knew Akira was onto something. That crazy idea back then had somehow shown a hope of light.

Kenji chuckled to himself now, remembering how unsure it had sounded back then. But they had done it. The sharks had kept the fish moving, alive and brimming with life. When they returned with their next haul, the transformation had been extraordinary. The villagers and buyers had been amazed - the fish looked as though they had just been pulled from the ocean.

Their gamble paid off. Word of their success spread across Japan, and the once-struggling fishermen became pioneers. What had started as a desperate idea had turned into an empire.

Kenji smiled, grateful for Akira's endless optimism. Without him, they would never have found that quote, and the idea that had changed everything might never have come to life.

Kenji's phone buzzed in his pocket, snapping him back to the present. It was Akira. "Kenji, where are you? We're waiting! Is everything okay?"

Kenji smiled, still lost in thought. "Sorry, Akira. I was just… thinking about everything. About how far we've come. It all came back to me just now."

On the other end of the line, there was a brief pause. Akira's voice softened. "Yeah… me too. Today's success means a lot, doesn't it?"

For a few moments, both men were silent, the weight of their journey settling between them. Kenji cleared his throat, not wanting to reveal how emotional he felt. "I'll be there in 30 minutes. See you soon, dear partner."

Ending the call, Kenji reflected on those words that had carried them through - "Man thrives oddly enough only in the presence of a challenging environment." They had overcome one challenge, but he knew the journey didn't stop there. Success, after all, was not a destination - it was a process. "So, what's next?" he murmured to himself, knowing full well that this victory was just the beginning.

(This story is inspired by an anonymous source. We do not claim any copyright or credits for it.)

Mindful Reflections: »

Life is a journey filled with challenges, both big and small, that only encourage us to grow and evolve. While it's natural to seek comfort in familiar routines, true growth lies just beyond the borders of our comfort zones.

As L. Ron Hubbard aptly said, "Man thrives oddly enough only in the presence of a challenging environment." This insight reminds us that adversity is not an obstacle but an essential ingredient for personal development.

Think back to the first time you stepped into a gym. You might have been nervous and intimidated by the idea of lifting weights that seemed impossible. Perhaps you failed repeatedly at first, struggling with what others around you made look effortless. But with persistence, determination, and the resolve not to give up, you eventually lifted that weight you once thought was beyond your ability.

Or consider the simple act of starting a morning walk or jog. On day one, you might have pushed yourself to walk briskly, only to feel your legs protest with discomfort. Yet, as the days passed and you continued to show up, what once felt challenging started to feel achievable - even enjoyable. Over time, walking briskly or jogging intermittently became second nature.

These physical examples illustrate a universal truth - progress is born from stepping outside our comfort zones. Whether your goal is fat loss, muscle gain, or simply adopting a healthier lifestyle, none of it is possible without embracing the challenges along the way.

The struggles we face are not barriers but bridges and opportunities to discover our strength, resilience, and potential. It is through these challenges that we experience growth, leading to greater happiness, fulfilment, and a sense of accomplishment. So, the next time you encounter a challenge, you might embrace it with open arms, knowing it's only and only to shape you into the best version of yourself.

Historically, human evolution has been driven by challenges. Early humans didn't discover fire or invent tools because they were comfortable - they did it out of necessity, driven by the need to survive in difficult conditions. In much the same way, our personal and professional lives are shaped by the challenges that push us to adapt, learn, and innovate. Challenges expand our boundaries, build our resilience, and foster creativity in ways that comfort zones simply cannot.

When we face challenges, we are forced to confront the unknown. This mindful experience of being in the unknown pushes us to be aware at times, leading us to think and act in new ways, expanding our comfort zones and increasing our capabilities.

Pushing Boundaries is the necessary process to reach the summit of all sections in our life. Every challenge we overcome makes us more resilient. The ability to bounce back from setbacks is crucial to both personal development and professional success. Have you noticed this? Adversity often forces us to think outside the box. When conventional methods fail, we are required to find creative solutions, which often leads to new ideas and breakthroughs. Overcoming difficult situations strengthens our self-belief.

The more challenges we face and conquer, the more confident we become in our ability to tackle future obstacles. Beware of comfort zones. While they offer a sense of safety, they also create stagnation. And who wants to drink stagnant water? Staying in a place where everything is predictable limits growth and makes it harder to embrace new opportunities. Many people avoid challenges because they fear failure or discomfort, but this mindset keeps them from realising their true potential.

But remember, expanding your comfort zone doesn't mean taking extreme risks or making radical changes. Instead, it's about gradually introducing small challenges into your life, allowing you to grow without feeling overwhelmed.

Life is not a rat race, even though you may have bills to pay, places to explore, children to educate, and a family to provide for. All of these responsibilities can be managed while maintaining peace of mind and living a harmonious life. The key is not to resist challenges.

Accepting challenges could be very peaceful. Whatever you resist will persist until you learn the lesson and move forward. Hence, accept and adapt. Challenges offer us opportunities to progress, grow, and face yet another challenge with renewed strength.

As we conclude, I invite you to participate in a simple self-reflection activity that would help you feel accomplished after reading this post.

1. Write down a small challenge you experienced in the past. How did you overcome it? If you remember the process clearly, write it down in bullet points.

2. Reflect on that moment. Breathe deeply and acknowledge what had seemed difficult. What was that exact thing that made you unhappy or uncomfortable with accepting this new, unknown challenge? No judgments here; this is your self-reflection activity, just to be aware.

3. Consider what qualities or skills within you were triggered. How did stepping out of your comfort zone help you grow? Make a note of these insights.

4. Now, what if these kinds of challenges come again, would you be better equipped?

This list reflects your inner growth. Remember, applying what you've learned to future challenges may not guarantee success, but it equips you with the tools to face adversity. Give it a go, embrace challenges with an open heart, and you will gradually expand your comfort zone, unlocking new levels of personal growth and fulfillment.

❖ ❖ ❖

"Wisdom is not in knowing everything, but in knowing yourself." - Prem Rawat

Have You Ever Googled the Definition of An Entrepreneur?

When we were recording this exact episode, no. 10, I couldn't help but feel a surge of excitement. The familiar surroundings of the music recording studio, with its rich acoustics and calming ambience, had indeed become our second home. Mukund, our ever-supportive recordist, was already in his element, adjusting the mics and sound levels as Sudeep and I got comfortable. Today's topic, being an Entrepreneur, was one we both knew intimately. We lived, breathed, and walked that winding path full of triumphs and struggles.

But let me tell you, the hours leading up to this recording were far from smooth. I had one of those days where every task seemed like an uphill battle. Zumba instructor registrations were pouring in because the discount code was expiring that same day, and my phone was lighting up with calls, WhatsApp messages, and unread notifications.

They were coming in faster than I could deal with. And just to make things more hectic, I had to attend my daughter's 10th-grade parent-teacher meeting, which was mandatory, with her final exams looming on the horizon.

Of course, it couldn't have been scheduled on any other day! To top it off, I had to submit an urgent proposal to a corporate client for a 3-month employee well-being program using mindfulness tools, and if I hadn't sent it by 2 PM, I would've lost the contract. So there I was, putting out fires left, right and centre.

And Sudeep? He was also in the thick of it, wrestling with a significant project escalation. His partner is brilliant with the technical aspects, but let's just say people skills aren't his strong suit. Sudeep, though, is the one with the patience of a saint (okay, maybe that's a bit of an exaggeration, but you get the point). He's the one who always manages to turn chaos into calm, no matter how high the stakes. And today, he was neck-deep in a client issue that kept spiralling out of control because, surprise, the client couldn't stop changing their requirements or whatever it was. Sounds familiar?

It wasn't the peaceful lead-up to a podcast recording we usually prefer! But despite the madness, this is what we do. Before we record any episode, we have this little ritual-giving ourselves 30 minutes to chat about the topic. It helps us reset and refocus. Sometimes, in the mornings, I, with my coffee and Sudeep, with his favourite tea. Other times, it's in the afternoons when we've ticked a few things off our endless to-do lists. It's our time to breathe, reflect and get into the right headspace for recording. After all, the best thing we can do for our listeners is to be fully present. The more mindful we are, the better we can deliver our best.

So, today's episode was particularly special because Sudeep would share his journey as an entrepreneur.

He began, his voice immediately drawing you in like it always does. It had that perfect blend of drama and warmth, making listeners feel like they were in the room with us.

"Shweta, it's hard to believe, but it's been almost 10 years since I started my entrepreneurial journey. Right after graduating from engineering, I was curious about running my own business. I had this picture in my head. It all seemed perfect: being my own boss, setting my schedule, leading meetings, having a team working for me, and, of course, making money. But some lessons, as we know, come the hard way.

Shweta, do you remember how growing up, we were always told to stay away from three kinds of people: politicians, lawyers, and police officers? Well, life threw me in the opposite direction and let me tell you, my experiences have been…eye-opening.

A client was excited about his startup journey and wanted us to build a software product. Everything seemed great at first. We agreed on a price, and he paid as promised, but there were constant changes! In every meeting, it was like, 'Oh, I don't like what we talked about last time, let's change it.' After months, we were nowhere near completion. We were supposed to build a room, but it was turning into a whole skyscraper! My team was stuck in this endless loop, and I got frustrated.

So, I finally confronted him, thinking we could clear things up. But instead, he exploded! He was already angry because he couldn't sell a single copy of the software, and suddenly, I was the scapegoat. Out of nowhere, he tells me, 'Sudeep, I'm going to file a fraud case against you for 10 lakhs!' I was stunned, Shweta. I mean, how did things spiral so out of control?

At first, I thought he was just venting. Surely, he wasn't serious. But then, a few days later, my dad called me, panicked, saying someone had come to our house and threatened to press charges. I was furious! I couldn't believe this guy dared to come to my home and bother my family.

Days passed, and things might have calmed down. But then, I got a call from a police inspector. The words are still clear in my mind: 'Sir, there's a case being filed against you. We might have to arrest you. Meet us within two days.' Shweta, I almost fell off my chair. I had only ever been to the police station for a passport verification. I had no clue how to handle this!

The next day, I reached out to everyone I knew. People suggested all sorts of things. Some offered to set things up, others told me to fight it in court. One lawyer friend said, 'Sudeep, don't even go. Nothing will happen.' But none of these options felt right. Ultimately, I followed my gut because I knew I hadn't done anything wrong. So, with fear and determination, I went to the police station.

There he was, my client, flanked by his towering, weightlifter brothers while I stood alone, feeling a mix of disbelief and determination. After an eternity of waiting, the police inspector finally strolled in, his irritation evident. 'Get this sorted. I've got better things to do,' she snapped, her tone making it clear she wasn't interested in the details.

What followed was a tennis game of arguments, where voices kept rising as we argued for hours. It was painfully clear that the inspector was siding with my client. As the situation escalated, a nagging thought crept into my mind: 'Did he bribe the inspector? Is this whole mess just to make things harder for me?' It felt like the entire system was stacked against me. But despite the storm of accusations and doubts, I forced myself to stay calm. I knew I was in the right, and I wasn't going to let fear cloud my judgement.

And then, Shweta, the inspector, hit me with this line: 'When you buy vegetables and don't like them, don't you ask for your money back?' I paused for a moment and said, 'Yes, madam, but not after you've eaten them and digested them.' Silence. She didn't know what to say. My client went quiet, too. Finally, I told him, 'Take the software in whatever state it's in.' He didn't want it- maybe he was just done with it or couldn't handle it anymore. We settled on the software and some amount of money, and that was that.

Walking out of that police station was… surreal. I felt a rush of mixed emotions, but the lesson I learned was priceless. Shweta, being an entrepreneur means you're on your own all the time. You fight your battles and you celebrate your victories. But if you don't follow your heart and your instincts, you're never going to grow. That's what this journey is about."

Sudeep's experience, especially so early in his entrepreneurial journey, was a tough one, navigating legal threats and difficult clients and standing his ground when everything seemed stacked against him. It's a testament to his resilience and ability to work mindfully through challenges that would have broken many. I still remember, sitting in that acoustic studio during the recording of this episode, I looked at him and said, "Sudeep, you're still running your business, right? How resilient is that you've never given up on being an entrepreneur!" We both laughed, but there was an understanding at that moment of just how deep his perseverance runs, which is essentially a very important trait you must have if you ever plan to run your own business.

Even now, when I reflect on Sudeep's story, it moves me. It makes me think about the misconceptions people often have about the lives of entrepreneurs versus those in traditional jobs. I've heard so many people with jobs say, "Business owners are so lucky; they can work whenever they want and don't have to answer to anyone." And on the flip side, I've heard business owners say, "People with jobs are the lucky ones; they know they'll get paid at the end of the month no matter what."

But the truth is, whether you're running a business or working a job, the key is to follow your heart. It's about understanding your values, your interests and what truly drives you. In the end, the most important thing is doing what feels right for you, no matter the challenges or the rewards.

Mindful Reflections: ⟫

Entrepreneurship is often romanticised as the ultimate dream - being your own boss, making your own rules, and carving out your own destiny. But what truly separates a theoretical entrepreneur from a practical one? It's not just about generating ideas; it's about making tough decisions while staying rooted in authenticity.

Being your own boss might sound empowering, but it demands certain essential qualities - untiring conviction, resilience, and an invincible, never-give-up attitude. The grind is real - the entitled responsibility of making decisions, the relentless pursuit of growth, and the discipline to stay motivated through it all. Opinions and advice from others will pour in, but the real challenge lies in filtering through the noise to make decisions that align with your personal values and vision.

One of the greatest lessons in entrepreneurship or life, for that matter, is the irreplaceable importance of listening to your heart. In a world that often prioritises metrics, profits, or external expectations, real success is found in staying true to your inner compass.

Whether you're leading a business or excelling in a job, the same truth applies - knowing your values, interests, and what genuinely drives you is the foundation of meaningful achievement.

At its core, life and entrepreneurship is about authenticity. The challenges or rewards you encounter are secondary to the fulfilment of living in alignment with your purpose. So, embrace the journey, listen to your heart, and trust that every decision you make is a step toward the life you're meant to create. Nothing can hold you back from becoming who you're meant to be.

Let's take a few minutes to reflect on the following to enhance your performance in everything you are doing professionally right now:

1. Identify Your Values - What are the three values or principles you hold most dearly in your personal and professional life? Write them down.

2. Define Your Vision - Where do you see yourself five years from now professionally? What does being successful look like for you? Journal down this description.

3. Align Your Actions - Think about a recent decision you made. Did it align with your values and vision? If not, what could you have done differently? Was it controllable? Self-reflect and be aware that, for now, that's it.

4. Listen to Your Heart - Close your eyes for a moment and ask yourself: What does my heart truly want? Write down your immediate thoughts. Stay with this question at least once a day.

5. Lastly, review your answers and use them as a guide to ensure your journey, whether in entrepreneurship or life, stays true to what matters most to you.

You are an original being; explore more to become the best version of YOU.

❖ ❖ ❖

"Be where you are; otherwise, you will miss your life." - Buddha

The notion of giving despite not having enough

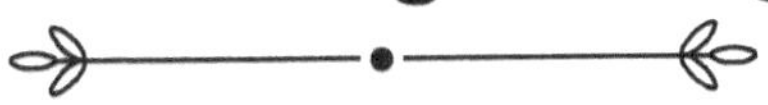

The morning fog lingered as the sun struggled to break through, casting a soft, almost nostalgic glow over Roopali. The cafe, with its timeless appeal, had become a second home for regulars like Rohan and Sanket.

Roopali sat on the bustling yet iconic Fergusson College Road, one of Pune's most famous streets. Despite being a one-way lane, the traffic there never seemed to catch a break - bikes, cars, and buses honked constantly, creating a steady hum that had become part of the cafe's soundtrack. Yet, amidst all the noise and chaos, FC Road retained its charm, with thick, old frangipani trees lining both sides, their branches stretching overhead to form a green canopy.

The usual clinking of cups, the hurried chatter of college students devouring dosas, and old men's loud, hearty laughter filled the air. Roopali hadn't changed a thing in what felt like centuries like time had paused for this place.

Its charm wasn't in its outdated interiors but in its authenticity. The cafe had an unspoken understanding with Pune's old-timers, a gathering spot for everyone to meet, share stories, and keep traditions alive.

Sanket, as usual, had already claimed their usual spot by the window, a glass of hot filter coffee in hand. His face was lost in thought until an old, shaky voice broke his concentration.

"Arey Sanket, today you're alone? Your friend didn't join you?" asked one of the cafe regulars, an elderly man known for striking up unsolicited conversations.

Sanket sighed, clearly not in the mood, but managed a polite reply. "Rohan's running late, Uncle. He'll be here soon." He forced a smile, his usual manners kicking in. "How are you, Uncle? You seem… extra happy today."

The old man, seizing the chance, shuffled over to Sanket's table, as if Sanket had invited him for a chat. "You know, you're right! My son from the Netherlands is finally visiting us after more than ten years! Can you believe it? He's married to a Dutch woman and has a five-year-old kid, all fair and lovely." His voice brimmed with joy, but Sanket's mind was elsewhere. He offered polite nods as the old man went on about the cold weather in the Netherlands and his wife's arthritis.

Just then, Rohan arrived, hurrying toward the table. He glanced at Sanket and the old man, shooting Sanket a playful look that said, Really, man? Are you chatting him up now?

The old man struggled to get up from their table, waving at Rohan as he did. "All good, beta. Everything's good!"

Rohan chuckled, returning to his usual spot, but not before throwing out another laugh.

Rohan smirked at Sanket, sliding into his spot. "Sanket, my dear friend, late one day and suddenly you're besties with Uncle over there? God bless you for finding such… quality company," he teased but quickly caught the severe look on Sanket's face.

"Rohan, I need to talk to you," Sanket said, his voice cutting through the usual hum of the café. There was a heaviness in his tone that immediately shifted the mood.

Rohan, still gesturing for his usual coffee, raised an eyebrow. "Everything okay, man?" he asked as the waiter set down his steaming glass of coffee.

Sanket didn't respond right away. His silence lingered, and Rohan could sense that this wouldn't be their usual light-hearted banter. The air between them felt heavier, contrasting with their usual ease.

Rohan, ever brimming with energy, thanks to his morning fitness routine, radiated positivity even in the stillness. Clad in his signature T-shirt and joggers, he was easy to spot, always looking ready to tackle the day head-on. His upright and confident posture reflected the discipline that came with running his personal training studio and IT business. The faint scent of sweat still clung to him, mixed with the familiar aroma of Roopali's strong filter coffee.

Sanket, on the other hand, looked worn out. His office job kept him tethered to the grind, draining him in ways Rohan's morning runs couldn't. His slightly slumped shoulders and weary eyes told the story of a man who rarely said "no," trapped in the obligations of his structured life. He wasn't as physically or mentally fit as Rohan, but these mornings at Roopali were his escape. The warm coffee, the earthy smell of wet pavement from the early morning mist, and the chatter of familiar faces grounded him, offering a brief respite from the weight of his daily routine.

Sanket exhaled deeply. "My younger brother got accepted for post-graduation abroad. Amazing news, but we need around 40-50 lakhs for his education."

Rohan's relaxed demeanour transformed as he leaned in, sensing the moment's gravity. Curious, he asked, "That's a significant amount, Sanket. How do you plan to gather that kind of money?"

He sighed, running a hand through his hair. "I've got an old bungalow in Khopoli, a village over 100 kilometres from Pune. No one's used it for years, except for a small family that lives there, taking care of the place. I've decided to sell it."

His voice was firm, but a flicker of doubt crossed his eyes. "I've made up my mind," he continued. "This is the only way. I need to ask the family living there to vacate."

The following weekend, Rohan, Sanket and his wife, Manasi, decided to take the trip together. Rohan insisted on driving his car, and they all climbed in for the journey to Khopoli, a serene village bordered by lush fields and cattle that grazed. The air was filled with farmland's rich, earthy aroma, offering a welcome escape from the city's hustle and bustle. They finally reached the old bungalow after a short search along the main road. It had been a while since Sanket last visited; his demanding job seldom allowed him a moment of peace, let alone the opportunity to relax on weekends, which were meant to be free of laptops and work calls.

It was a simple house, worn with time but maintained decently. Shivange, the caretaker, came out to greet us. He was a lean man, his skin weathered by the sun, but his eyes were kind and welcoming. "Namaste, Sir," he said with a warm smile, inviting everyone in and respectfully touching Sanket's feet.

Everyone sat on the cool stone floor. His wife, a quiet woman, brought them water and some gud - jaggery. "Jaggery helps to cool down the heat, you know?" Rohan whispered to Sanket, trying to lighten the mood. Rohan's eyes wandered around the house. The place was crumbling. There was no furniture, no bed - just bare floors. Shivange's family lived in utter simplicity. His wife and two small children peeked from the corner, and an old woman, his mother, lay on a tattered mat in the corner, clearly unwell.

Sanket's face reflected his apprehension; this would not be easy. Meanwhile, Manasi wore a casual, carefree expression as she stepped out of the house to take a call from a friend. After a few minutes, Rohan and Sanket decided to go for a walk just as Manasi returned to the bungalow, saying she would check with Shivange's wife about the dinner preparations. The village was tranquil, with the evening sun casting a warm, golden glow over the fields.

That night, they all sat down for dinner. It was a simple meal—rice, dal, and a vegetable curry. Despite their apparent hardships, Shivange was cheerful, his face lit up with excitement. "Sir, it's such a pleasure to have you here," he said, almost joyfully. This year, I planted carrots, but the rains didn't come. The crop failed."

He kept talking, his words flowing easily, while we quietly listened, nodding occasionally. After the meal, Rohan pulled Sanket aside. "Sanket, you can't sell this house. Look at them. They have nowhere to go. They need more time."

Sanket looked conflicted. "I know Rohan, but I need the money. How else can I help my brother?"

Understanding the weight of the situation and how crucial it was for Sanket to gather the money for his brother's education, especially with their father being retired for years, Rohan paused before speaking. "You know, I've just sold some land I inherited from my mother's side and set aside some money. How about I lend it to you? You can pay me back when things settle down. There's no need to sell this house right now."

He looked at me, surprised but grateful. "You'd do that?" he asked quietly. "I don't know how to thank you, Rohan."

Just as they finished their conversation, the door creaked, and Shivange stood with a pile of mattresses. He smiled, quietly setting them up for everyone. Rohan then realised that Shivange had probably overheard everything. But he said nothing and kept that gentle smile on his face as he ensured we were comfortable for the night.

The following day, as Rohan settled into the driver's seat and they were preparing to leave, Shivange hurried over, stopping them just as Sanket was listening to Manasi, who was showing something on her phone. "Sir, please wait,"

Shivange called out, holding a bunch of vibrant orange carrots neatly tied with a red ribbon. "These are fresh from the market. Madam can make halwa with them."

They politely tried to decline, but Shivange gently placed them into Manasi's hands, insisting. The carrots were flawless, freshly tied and beautifully arranged. Watching from the driver's seat, Rohan felt an unexpected lump form in his throat.

While driving home, Rohan could not stop thinking about those carrots Shivange had placed in Manasi's hand. Where had he gotten them? He said his crop had failed. Then, as Rohan turned around the bus stop to get out of the village towards the highway, he saw a small market on the road. Vendors were selling carrots exactly like the ones he had given us, tied with red ribbons. He had bought them just for Sanket and Manasi.

Rohan gently turned to Sanket, who was sitting next to him. Their eyes met, and exactly the same thought lingered on their minds, both of them taken aback. Here was a man with nothing, and yet he had gone out of his way to offer us something.

As they navigated the bumpy stretch of road, their bodies jolting with each uneven turn, the silence in the car seemed to echo the weight of their unspoken thoughts. The only sound was Kishore Kumar's melodies playing softly in the background. Suddenly, Sanket's wife's phone rang, breaking the quiet. She tapped Sanket's shoulder, gesturing for him to lower the volume. As the music faded, she answered the call, already deep in conversation with a friend, discussing the best way to make gajar ka halwa.

It's easy to give when you have plenty. But to give when you have so little, that's a rare kind of kindness. That day, both Sanket and Rohan realised they had made the right decision for the right man. Though Rohan's help wouldn't fully cover the 40 to 50 lakhs Sanket needed, it eased some of the burden. Sanket knew he'd have to dip into his savings for the rest, which stirred tension at home, with Manasi unhappy about his choice. Yet, Sanket found a strange sense of calm, refusing to let the temporary conflict disturb his peace. As Manasi invited her friends over to help make gajar ka halwa, Sanket sat quietly, reflecting on the sacrifices made for the family and the moments of grace that followed.

(This story is inspired by the works of writer and stand-up comedian Sanket Joshi. We do not claim any copyright or credits for it.)

Mindful Reflections: 》》

Innately, human existence lies in the simple concept of giving. Whether it's knowledge passed down, wisdom shared, or material resources offered to others, giving forms the foundation of our connections with one another. In today's fast-paced world, giving can take many forms - sharing skills, providing tangible support, or offering non-material gifts like appreciation, love, empathy, and compassion. Each act of generosity not only strengthens our relationships but also fills our lives with a deep sense of purpose and fulfilment.

But the true test of generosity reveals itself when we have little to give. When resources are scarce; be it time, energy, or wealth, can we still give wholeheartedly, or do we hesitate? As the popular saying goes, "Whenever you give, give wholeheartedly and without hesitation." It's easy to be generous when you have plenty. But when you're struggling yourself, that's when the act of giving becomes truly meaningful.

Giving from the heart, especially in times of personal scarcity, demonstrates a rare form of kindness; one that leaves a lasting impact. It's not about the quantity or value of what you give; it's about the intent behind it. The more we give, the more we feel a sense of purpose. What good is holding on to knowledge or material wealth if we can't share it for the greater good?

Consider moments when someone comforted you, even when they themselves were going through a difficult time. Or perhaps a stranger showed you a small act of kindness when you least expected it. These gestures, made without expectation or reward, hold immense value because they come from a place of selflessness. The giver isn't looking for recognition; they give simply because they want to contribute, even when they have little to spare.

When we embrace this mindset, the act of giving becomes transformative, both for the giver and the receiver. It reflects gratitude, deepens connections, and creates a ripple effect of positivity that touches the lives of many.

How can we cultivate this spirit of giving in our own lives? It starts with recognizing that generosity doesn't always require grand gestures or material wealth. Sometimes, the smallest acts; like a kind word, a listening ear, or a moment of understanding, are the most meaningful. It's about being present, giving from the heart, and doing so without expectation.

Let's experience this power of giving from the heart by experimenting with this simple activity. Take 5 minutes today and think about someone in your life who could benefit from an act of kindness. It doesn't have to be someone close to you, it could be a colleague, a neighbour, or even a stranger.

1. What is something small yet meaningful that you could offer? It could be your time, a word of encouragement, or even just a smile.

2. Take a deep breath, and with genuine intent, go ahead and give without any expectation of something in return.

3. After you've done this, reflect on how it made you feel. Did it shift your mood or perspective in any way?

The beauty of giving is that it's not about how much you have; it's about how much you're willing to share from the heart. Ultimately isn't life about giving and transferring knowledge to the next generation?

"Drink your tea slowly and reverently, as if it is the axis on which the world revolves."
– Thích Nhất Hạnh

Relationships is the crucial content to the recipe of life

Rahul was the kind of kid who thrived on laughter, games, and the company of friends. He could run for hours, play until his legs gave out, and still want more. But when it came to books and homework, his energy fizzled out. By the time he reached 8th standard, his midterm results had dropped, enough to make his mother's temper burst.

"You're not even trying, Rahul!" she scolded, her voice filled with irritation. "If you don't shape up now, how do you expect to pass? You're going to tuition, no more arguments!"

So, reluctantly, Rahul found himself shuffling into a new tuition class, his stomach knotting with nerves. The room smelled faintly of chalk and old textbooks. He scanned the unfamiliar faces, awkwardly tugging at the straps of his bag, unsure of where to sit. That's when he noticed

Siddharth, sitting calmly at the back, his head resting casually against the wall.

Siddharth had a certain ease about him, an air of quiet confidence that Rahul immediately found comforting. They exchanged a quick smile, and within minutes, it was like they'd known each other for years.

"What's your favourite subject?" Siddharth asked as they walked home together after class that day.

"Favourite?" Rahul laughed. "I barely survive them! But maybe history… on a good day."

Siddharth chuckled. "Yeah, I get that. History's cool. But maths? It's a nightmare."

From that day forward, they walked to tuition together, their conversations meandering from school gossip to their favourite snacks. Stopping at the corner shop for icy Pepsi Colas became their shared tradition, the fizzy sweetness providing the perfect antidote to the dullness of the classroom.

At home, Rahul had another friend, his sleek, graceful cat, a creature he adored. The cat would curl up beside him as he studied, her soft purring a soothing background sound. But one day, as Rahul watched his cat finish her bowl of milk, a scrappy little kitten appeared out of nowhere. The tiny creature waited, its eyes wide and hopeful, before sneaking up to lap up the leftover milk.

"Hey, shoo!" Rahul waved his hands, annoyed. "This is my cat's milk. Get lost!"

But the kitten returned the next day. And the day after that.

No matter how many times Rahul chased it away, the persistent little thing kept coming back.

One afternoon, after class, Rahul brought Siddharth over to his house.

"Come meet my cat," Rahul said, his voice bright with excitement. "She's the queen around here."

Siddharth knelt down to stroke the cat, who purred in contentment. Just then, the kitten appeared again, creeping toward the empty bowl.

"Not you again," Rahul groaned, standing up to chase it away. But before he could move, Siddharth gently caught his wrist.

"Wait," Siddharth said, looking at the kitten with a soft smile. "Where's it supposed to go? It's just hungry."

Rahul hesitated, feeling torn between his loyalty to his cat and Siddharth's kindness. "But this one isn't even ours. It's just… stealing."

Siddharth shrugged. "Then why don't we give it its own bowl? There's plenty of milk, right?"

Rahul blinked, surprised by the suggestion. "But if my mom finds out I'm feeding two cats, she'll flip!"

"Let's do it anyway," Siddharth said with a grin. "Come on, it'll be fun."

Sighing but unable to resist Siddharth's enthusiasm, Rahul went to the kitchen and poured a fresh bowl of milk for the kitten. The scrappy little creature eagerly lapped it up while Siddharth watched, his smile widening.

From then on, their after-school routine included both cats. Rahul's house became their playground, where they'd chase the kitten, laugh as it scurried away, and spend hours just playing with the two feline companions. Those were the best days, carefree and full of simple joys.

Then, one week, Siddharth stopped showing up for tuition. At first, Rahul thought nothing of it, maybe Siddharth was sick or busy with family. But when days turned into a full week, worry crept in.

On the sixth day, Rahul approached their tuition teacher. "Ma'am, do you have Siddharth's phone number? He hasn't been coming, and I'm a little worried."

The teacher nodded, concern engraved on her face. "He hasn't missed a single class before this. Here, take his number. Let me know if you find anything."

Rahul rushed home, his heart thudding with anxiety. Dialling Siddharth's number, he felt a cold sweat trickle down his spine. The phone rang twice before a soft, feminine voice answered.

"Hello?"

"Hi, aunty, this is Rahul. Is Siddharth there? He hasn't been coming to class…"

"Oh, Rahul, beta," Siddharth's mother sighed. "He's not well. He's been resting. I'll tell him you called."

Relief washed over Rahul, but it was mixed with a lingering unease. Siddharth was sick, yes, but something about his absence felt off, like there was more beneath the surface. Still, Rahul didn't push. He'd wait. He just hoped his friend would be back to his old self soon.

When Siddharth finally returned to tuition, something had changed. His usual warmth had faded, replaced by a quiet, distant demeanour that was disturbing to Rahul. Gone were the easy smiles and carefree chatter. No matter how much Rahul tried to persuade it out of him, Siddharth remained closed off, his silence a wall between them.

It wasn't until one evening, after class, when Rahul was held back by the teacher to discuss his test results, that he found Siddharth walking home alone. Rahul hurried after him, his chappals slapping against the pavement, and called out, "Hey, Siddharth! What's going on? Why didn't you wait for me?"

Siddharth stopped but didn't turn around. After a pause, he said in a low voice, "Rahul… everything's changed. I don't know who I am anymore."

Rahul furrowed his brows, stepping closer. "What are you talking about?"

And then, like a dam breaking, the truth poured out. Siddharth had recently discovered that he was adopted. His parents had kept it from him all his life waiting for the right age to inform him the same, and the revelation now felt like a betrayal, cracking open his sense of identity. He was tormented by questions, who were his real parents, and why had they given him up? His adoptive mother, the woman he had loved and trusted, refused to tell him more, saying it didn't matter. But for Siddharth, it did. The secrecy gnawed at him, making him feel like a stranger in his own family.

Rahul didn't know what to say. He could see the pain in his friend's eyes, the uncertainty that clouded every moment.

Siddharth barely paid attention in class, his mind somewhere far away.

One evening, in a rare moment of vulnerability, Siddharth asked, "Can I stay at your place tonight? I just need to get away."

Rahul nodded. "Of course, man. Stay as long as you need."

That night, they did their best to forget everything, laughing, playing games, sharing inside jokes that momentarily brought Siddharth back to his old self. But as the dawn crept in, their fragile bubble of normalcy burst with a sharp knock on the door.

Rahul's mom opened it to find Siddharth's parents standing outside. His mother's eyes were red and puffy from crying. "Where have you been, Siddharth?" she asked, her voice trembling. "You didn't tell us anything. We've been so worried."

Siddharth's face tightened with frustration. "You don't understand," he muttered. "I feel like I'm trapped. You keep telling me to move on, but how can I when you won't give me answers?"

His mother reached out, but Siddharth stepped back, his emotions churning. Rahul watched helplessly, feeling the tension crackle between them.

Days passed again without Siddharth in class. Then, one afternoon, while Rahul was walking alone to tuitions he saw him standing outside their usual spot, the corner shop where they always stopped for Pepsi Colas. Siddharth had a different energy about him, lighter, as if a weight had been lifted.

"Let's skip class today," Siddharth said, grinning for the first time in weeks.

They sat at the shop, the familiar hiss of soda bottles filling the air, and Siddharth finally told Rahul what had happened. After days of searching, he had gone to the orphanage where he had been adopted. Persistent inquiries led him to meet his birth mother, who still worked there as a cleaning lady.

"When I saw her," Siddharth said, his voice calm, "I thought everything would fall into place. But… it didn't. She was just another person. She put her hand on my head, but there was no rush of recognition, no grand moment. She was a stranger. It made me realise that my real parents are the ones who raised me, the ones who've been there every day."

Rahul nodded, understanding the gravity of the realisation. "So… what now?"

Siddharth smiled softly, the storm inside him finally settling. As they got up to leave, Siddharth turned to Rahul with a small, hopeful grin. "Hey, can I ask you something?"

"Sure," Rahul said, raising an eyebrow.

"Can I adopt that kitten?"

Rahul's face lit up with a wide grin. "Of course! She's yours," he said, secretly relieved that he wouldn't have to face his mom's scoldings about feeding a second cat anymore.

And in that moment, as they walked back home with Pepsi Colas in hand and a kitten waiting for a new home, Siddharth felt like he was closing one chapter of his life and stepping into another, one where love, family, and identity didn't need to be as complicated as he once thought.

It was a beginning filled with acceptance, new bonds, and the promise of brighter days ahead.

Mindful Reflections: »

As human beings, we are naturally social creatures. Our evolution has been shaped by relationships, social bonding, and community, and these connections continue to be vital to our existence. While relationships can sometimes feel like a burden, they are also what make life meaningful. Without them, we lose a fundamental part of what it means to be human.

In our lives, we all create an inner circle of people; the ones closest to us, the ones we trust the most. These are the people who know our stories, share in our joys and struggles, and accept us as we are. Yet, how often do we take a moment to acknowledge their importance? How often do we express gratitude for their presence in our lives?

It's easy to take these relationships for granted. Whether it's family, close friends, or even a partner, we sometimes assume they know how much we value them without saying it. But love and connection grow stronger when we recognize them openly.

Take a moment to think about the people in your life who mean the most to you; not just your family or best friends, but perhaps someone unexpected who has had a deep impact on you. Could you make a list of at least five people who are incredibly valuable to you, who accept you just as you are? And once you've made that list, take this moment to express your gratitude. Send them a message, give them a call, or simply tell them how much they mean to you.

Gratitude is a simple act, but it has the power to nurture and preserve the relationships that enrich our lives. It reminds us that we're never alone, and that our connections, no matter how small, are what give life its emotional depth and meaning. So, let's not wait for a special occasion. Let's express gratitude to those who matter most, and keep the bonds that hold us together strong. Today let's not forget to honour the people who add love, support, and emotional essence to our lives.

"When the mind is pure, joy follows like a shadow that never leaves." - Buddha

Do you accept yourself?

Vaidehi had always been a quiet force of resilience. In her early 40s, she expertly balanced the demands of raising her almost teenage son while managing a high-stakes corporate job on the 18th floor of Dwarka Towers, a gleaming glass giant in the heart of Bangalore. Her days were a delicate choreography; morning school runs filled with her son's laughter, followed by back-to-back conference calls echoing through the barren office corridors, and finally, tender bedtime stories shared in the soft glow of the night.

"Mom, can you read me one more?" her son Ravi would plead, his wide eyes glittering with innocence.

"Just one more, and then it's lights out," she'd reply, ruffling his hair, her heart swelling with love.

Despite the challenges that came with single motherhood, Vaidehi radiated warmth and conviction. Colleagues admired her sharp ethics and principles; her presence was a soothing balm in the frenetic corporate atmosphere. Yet beneath her composed exterior lay an undercurrent of solitude, a whisper of doubt that lurked in the corners of her mind.

But fate had a different script in mind for her, one that was about to turn her world upside down.

It was a Friday afternoon, and the sun poured through the office windows, casting long shadows on the polished floor. The clatter of keyboards and hushed conversations filled the air as Vaidehi focused on her work, her fingers dancing over the keys. Suddenly, a deafening crack shattered the mundane hum of the office.

"Did you hear that?" her colleague, Priya, asked, her voice tinged with concern.

Before Vaidehi could respond, the lights flickered ominously, and a deafening alarm blared through the building. Panic gripped the air like a vice as the fire alarm wailed, drowning out the frantic shouts echoing down the corridor.

"Evacuate! Now!" came a voice over the intercom.

Vaidehi's heart raced as she watched the chaos unfold. Flames began to lick the walls, hungry and alive, creeping upward with terrifying speed.

"Stay low!" she shouted to Priya, but the words were barely audible over the growing roar of the fire.

Smoke billowed into the room, thick and suffocating. Vaidehi's lungs burned as she crouched beneath her desk, her heart thundering in her chest.

"People are jumping!" Priya exclaimed, her eyes wide with terror as she peered out the window.

"Are you crazy? We can't jump from the 18th floor!" Vaidehi responded, panic lacing her voice. The view from the window, once a picturesque cityscape, now felt like a cruel reminder of their entrapment.

As the smoke thickened, the world around her dissolved into darkness. Thoughts of her children raced through her mind. What would happen to them if I don't make it out alive?

The acrid scent of burning material stung her nostrils, and she could feel the heat of the flames as they danced closer. Suddenly, a faint voice broke through the haze.

"Is anyone here?"

"Help! We're here!" Vaidehi wanted to scream, but her throat was raw, choked with smoke.

Just as despair threatened to consume her, she felt a presence. A figure emerged from the swirling smoke, a firefighter.

"Grab my leg!" he shouted, his voice booming over the chaos.

With a surge of strength, she reached out, her hand clutching the fabric of his pants. He pulled her closer, shouting for backup as he guided her through the acrid air.

The descent was agonisingly slow. Each step down the stairs felt like an eternity, the smoke curling around her like a living thing. Darkness enveloped her, and just as she felt herself slipping away, the world faded to black.

When Vaidehi awoke, the rhythmic beeping of machines filled her ears, a stark contrast to the chaos of the fire. Blinking against the harsh lights of the ICU, she tried to speak, but nothing came out. Her voice was gone, her lungs ravaged by the smoke.

"Mommy, please wake up!" Ravi's voice echoed in her mind, a haunting melody of love and desperation.

For nearly three weeks, she remained in a coma, her children and her father a retired army officer keeping vigil at her bedside, their hands wrapped in prayer. When she finally opened her eyes, the world around her felt alien.

"Vaidehi! Thank God you're awake!" her father exclaimed, tears glistening in his eyes.

"Where… am I?" she rasped, her voice a mere whisper, strained and unfamiliar.

"You're in the hospital, sweetheart. You survived," he said, his voice breaking with emotion.

But the road ahead was steep. The doctors explained the extent of her injuries; her vocal cords had been destroyed, and recovery would take months.

Though she fought to regain her strength, Vaidehi felt like a shadow of her former self. The nurses joked about her extended stay, but each jest felt like a dagger in her heart. The fire had stolen more than her voice; it had robbed her of her identity.

When she finally returned home, the mirror became her enemy. As she stood before it, she saw a stranger; her once-familiar face now scarred and burned, her spirit dulled.

With tears streaming down her cheeks, she whispered to herself, "Would it have been better to die that day?"

But then she turned, catching sight of Ravi, diligently studying at the kitchen table. His presence ignited a flicker of hope within her. She remembered those who had perished, the colleagues and friends who wouldn't get a second chance. She was alive, and for that, she felt grateful.

"I have to honour them," she thought, determination flooding her veins.

One afternoon, she called Ravi over, her voice trembling but resolute. "Ravi, I want to arrange a small event at Dwarka Towers. Will you help me?"

"Of course, Mom," he replied, his smile reassuring. "We'll do it together."

Together, they organised a memorial for the survivors and families of those lost in the fire. On the day of the event, Vaidehi returned to the building for the first time since the disaster. The once grand office lay in ruins, charred and blackened, a stark reminder of the horror that had unfolded within its walls.

As she stood where her desk had been, she whispered a quiet thank you to the universe.

"Thank you for letting me live," she murmured, her heart swelling with emotion.

Survivors and families gathered, their voices a mixture of grief and resilience, sharing stories, shedding tears, and keeping alive the memories of those lost. Each tale wove a tapestry of love and pain, binding everyone together in their shared tragedy. As Vaidehi stood amidst them, a quiet transformation began within her. She understood now that her survival had a purpose. Though her scars, both visible and hidden, would forever mark her, they no longer felt like a burden but a testament to her endurance.

With renewed strength, Vaidehi left that day with a deep sense of resolve. The fire may have stolen her voice, but it had not extinguished her spirit. Her heart, though battered, still beat with purpose. She had been given a second chance, not just to survive, but to live fully. And now, she was ready to embrace her future with courage, grace and acceptance, no longer defined by the fire that tried to break her, but by the life she chose to rebuild in its aftermath.

(This story is inspired by the works of author Sudha Murthy. We do not claim any copyright or credits for it.)

Mindful Reflections: »

Have you ever found yourself asking:

Why am I the way I am?

Why don't I look a certain way?

Why am I not tall enough?

Why don't I meet society's beauty standards?

Why isn't my skin lighter?

These questions are part of the human experience, constantly fueled by the influences that surround us, media, culture, and societal expectations. We've all been there, questioning our worth based on external factors. It's natural to feel this way, but living a fulfilled and joyful life begins with one powerful step – self-acceptance.

Imagine, instead of constantly striving to meet these unreal ideals, you simply said, "I accept myself. I love myself. I am enough."

But here's the hard truth – we often lie to ourselves, pretending that we don't care about these things, or worse, we suppress the hurt they cause. What if, instead of denying, you embraced a life rooted in self-acceptance?

In this space, we're going to explore what self-acceptance truly looks like, even when life takes a turn for the worst. It's easy to feel empowered when things are going well, but when your world turns upside down, self-love feels nearly impossible. There are moments when accepting oneself seems impossible, but remember that's exactly the path to healing, confidence and empowerment.

As you reflect on this, I invite you to engage in a meaningful activity: Ask yourself, "What if I met ME? Would I fall in love with ME?"

Think about it, not the version of you that others see, but the real, raw, imperfect you. Would you embrace yourself with the same compassion and kindness you offer others? Because self-acceptance isn't just a buzzword; it's the foundation of a genuinely happy and fulfilling life. The moment you fully accept yourself, you unlock a life of peace, purpose, and freedom.

As humans, we are naturally wired to progress. If we achieve a certain body shape, we want a better one. If we reach one career summit, we aim for the next. It's this drive for "more" that propels us forward, and often, success follows. But the pursuit of more means little if it's built on a foundation of self-sabotage and self-criticism.

The only way to move forward successfully is by accepting

yourself as you are right now. Be grateful for the person you are in this moment. From this place of self-acceptance, explore the deeper intent behind your existence if you wish to grow. It's from this high-vibe mindset that you can set new self-improvement goals, not from a place of lack, but from a place of love and self-worth.

So, let's begin this journey today. One day at a time, one step at a time. Embrace who you are now, and watch how that self-acceptance fuels your growth toward who you would want to become.

❖ ❖ ❖

"Mindfulness is a process of actively noticing new things. It creates energy and joy."
- Ellen Langer

The only way is to empower yourself

Berlin was a city cloaked in the shadows of its former glory. Once a symbol of vibrancy and power, it now lay in ruins, its streets silent and cold, mirroring the despair of its people. World War I had left deep scars, and the Treaty of Versailles had sealed Germany's humiliation, stripping it of pride, territory, and military might. The soul of the city was fractured, its bustling avenues reduced to memories of a brighter past.

Amidst the rubble, two men stood as symbols of their nation's plight. One, a middle-aged man with worry etched into every line of his face, shook his head in disbelief. "No air force, no army worth its name, and a debt so massive our grandchildren will still be paying for it," he muttered bitterly.

His wiry companion exhaled a plume of smoke, the cigarette trembling between his fingers. "It's not just the debt. The treaty was designed to crush us forever. They don't even hide it. The Allied nations could walk into Berlin today and remind us we're nothing."

The first man gave a bitter laugh. "Might as well let them spank us while they're at it."

But not all in Berlin were resigned to despair. In the shadows of the city stood a man with a fiery determination and a peculiar moustache - Adolf Hitler. A soldier who had fought in the trenches of World War I, the defeat of his homeland left a wound that refused to heal. To Hitler, the Treaty of Versailles was more than an agreement; it was a dagger thrust into Germany's soul. And he vowed to pull it out, no matter the cost.

"The treaty was a betrayal!" he thundered in beer halls and public squares, his words brimming with rage and conviction. Crowds began to gather, drawn by the power of his fiery oratory. "Germany will rise again! I will restore her glory!" Some laughed at him, dismissing his impassioned cries as the ramblings of a dreamer. But Hitler, unfazed, lashed out at his skeptics. "Laugh now," he sneered. "But follow me if you want your children to live in a powerful Germany, one they can be proud of!"

His words ignited a spark in the hearts of the disheartened. Pride that had been buried under years of defeat began to stir. "Perhaps he's the one," people whispered. "Perhaps he can save us."

By 1923, Hitler's influence had grown, and emboldened by his following, he staged a coup - the Beer Hall Putsch. It ended in failure, and he was arrested. Yet, his time in prison only cemented his image as a man willing to sacrifice for Germany's future. His writings and speeches, smuggled out and spread widely, turned him into a symbol of defiance against the Treaty of Versailles and the status quo.

By 1933, the tides of politics and public opinion turned in his favor. President Hindenburg, under immense pressure, reluctantly appointed him Chancellor. What many viewed as a routine political compromise, Hitler saw as destiny fulfilled. Alone in his office, he stared into a mirror, his reflection unflinching. "Germany needs me," he murmured. "And I will not fail her."

With power firmly in his grasp, Hitler dismantled Germany's fragile democracy, replacing it with a dictatorship bent on conquest. But he was not alone in his ambitions. In Italy, Benito Mussolini was rising, driven by similar dreams of restoring his nation's former greatness. Their shared disdain for the postwar order brought them together. Over glasses of wine in a lavish hall, Mussolini smirked. "Our nations have suffered long enough."

Hitler raised his glass in agreement. "The world will soon know who truly holds power."

Their alliance was forged, and soon, Japan joined their ranks, driven by its own imperial aspirations. Together, they formed the Axis Powers, a coalition born not of trust but of shared ambition.

Defying the Treaty of Versailles step by step, Hitler rebuilt Germany's military, created an air force, and marched troops into the forbidden Rhineland. The Allies, hesitant and divided, watched but did nothing. Encouraged by their inaction, Hitler pushed further. In 1938, he annexed

Austria without a single shot fired.

"What's next?" his generals asked eagerly.

"Czechoslovakia," he replied with a chilling grin.

The Allies, desperate to avoid another war, attempted to appease him. They allowed him to take parts of Czechoslovakia in exchange for a promise of peace. British Prime Minister Neville Chamberlain returned home waving the agreement, declaring, "Peace for our time!" But Hitler's words meant nothing. Within months, all of Czechoslovakia was under his control.

In 1939, when Germany invaded Poland, the world could no longer stand idle. France, still reveling in its World War I victory, was stunned as German troops marched into Paris. The Axis Powers, united by a shared lust for domination, had plunged the world into chaos.

The fragile peace was shattered, replaced by a conflict that consumed nations and scarred humanity. This was not merely a story of war; it was a tale of unchecked ambition, betrayal, and a lust for power that redefined the course of history.

The world teetered on the edge of destruction, its fate shaped by the ambitions of a few. In their pursuit of power, Hitler, Mussolini, and Japan ignited a firestorm that still serves as a stark reminder of the cost of greed and the courage needed to resist it. This chapter of history, written in blood and sacrifice, remains a warning to us all.

(This story is inspired by an anonymous source. We do not claim any copyright or credits for it.)

Mindful Reflections: 》

Life often feels like a game of power – either we strive to wield it, or we follow those who do. Power subtly shapes our decisions, guiding us toward choices that may or may not always align with our true desires. History is filled with compelling stories of humanity's relentless pursuit of power, but this chase has often led to great destruction, hasn't it?

In our daily lives, power manifests in many forms – through our roles, identities, and relationships. We assert power when we offer unsolicited advice, impose commands, or seek control over others and situations. Have you noticed that when we feel disempowered or weak, we often turn to labels – like being a boss, a parent, or someone with strong opinions or a louder voice – to reclaim control? Why do we behave this way, often without consciously thinking about it?

The answer lies in our inherent human nature – we all have an unconscious desire to seek power. This drive varies based on our individual values, desires, and interests. For instance, a million-follower social media influencer might not seem powerful to someone who isn't invested in social media. However, a professional speaker – someone whose expertise lies in leadership or training – might be seen as more powerful by the same person. Power is not one-size-fits-all; it's shaped by what we value and where our interests lie.

But here's the crucial question – Is this the life you truly want to live? A life shaped by external power, or one that comes from within?

Now, picture this instead – a life where your power isn't defined by controlling others, but by the mastery you hold over yourself. However, it often feels easier to exert control over those who seem weaker, rather than investing the energy needed for personal growth and self-mastery. It's tempting to think that you can make better decisions for those whose personalities are still developing, but that won't bring true fulfillment. True power comes from leading with wisdom, staying motivated, and taking purposeful actions that propel you toward your fullest potential - a life of continuous progress and self-development. That is the essence of real power.

This shift isn't about rejecting power; it's about redefining it. True power comes from within. It's the ability to conquer your fears, overcome self-doubt, and fuel your journey with passion and purpose. It's about serving others, contributing your unique skills, and making an impact that transcends the superficial chase for control.

The more we try to dominate others - whether it's employees, children, or spouses - the more we limit our own true power. What will you gain by controlling those who either fear or love you, and who obey you to avoid hurting you? Taking control over others, deciding what they should do according to your own values and beliefs, won't fulfill your life's purpose. Instead, what if you channeled that energy inward, to design your own life?

True contentment comes when you guide your loved ones, empower your employees to reach their highest potential, and contribute to society using the skills you've been gifted. This is where a mindful, abundant mindset emerges - because life is filled with limitless opportunities for all of us.

Remember this - You are alive right now, and this one life is your greatest opportunity. Don't let it slip away chasing illusions of power. Instead, channel your energy to grow, to serve, and to make every moment count. Live a life that not only fulfills you but also inspires those around you.

Are you ready to redefine your power and step into your highest potential? Welcome to this high-vibe, energetic, and liberating space. Let your journey begin!

❖ ❖ ❖

"Every breath is a gift. Every moment is an opportunity." - Prem Rawat

Is your life passion driven?

As a child, he wasn't just a moviegoer; he was a wide-eyed dreamer, captivated by the stories that unfolded on the big screen. The dimming of the theatre lights, the flickering of the projector, and the first strains of the soundtrack were pure enchantment. Every trip to the cinema was an event; a sacred ritual. He would sit on the edge of his seat, his heart racing in sync with the film's twists and turns. Heroes and villains became larger-than-life figures in his young mind, their journeys sparking something deep within him.

In his small, bustling neighbourhood in the fast-paced city of Mumbai, films were more than entertainment; they were an escape. The characters on screen spoke of worlds he had never seen, emotions he yearned to understand, and dreams he longed to chase. He would often recount scenes to his friends, mimicking dialogues and gestures, his voice brimming with excitement. For him, the screen wasn't just a window into stories - it was a mirror reflecting his hidden aspirations.

But the real turning point came in 1986 when he watched 'Naam'. It wasn't just a film; it was an experience that changed him. The emotional depth of the story, the magnetic performances, and the haunting soundtrack resonated with him in ways he couldn't fully explain. As the end credits rolled, he sat still, unwilling to leave his seat, his mind ablaze with thoughts. It was as if the film had awakened something dormant within him - a voice that whispered, "This is where you belong. This is what you must do."

That evening, as he walked home under the orange glow of streetlights, his usual chatter was replaced by quiet determination. He didn't know how or when, but he was certain of one thing - acting wasn't just a dream - it was his calling. The journey ahead seemed daunting, almost impossible, but the boy who left the cinema that night carried with him a spark that no hardship could extinguish.

From that day forward, his love for films transformed into a deep passion for storytelling. He would sit eyes glued to the screen, watching the iconic dialogues of Amitabh Bachchan in films like 'Sholay', 'Deewaar', and 'Zanjeer'. He mimicked every line with precision, especially Bachchan's intense delivery of "Main aaj bhi uss sheher mein hoon… jahan pe sab kuch badal gaya hai" from 'Deewaar'. He stood tall in front of the mirror, imitating every gesture, from the way Bachchan clenched his fist in anger to the slight pause in his voice that commanded attention.

His middle-class Mumbai household became his stage, and his mirror, the audience. He'd practice acting out dialogues from 'Naam' too, where the tension between love, loss, and the search for redemption was palpable in every word spoken by the characters. He'd try to replicate the emotion in the voice of Kumar Gaurav as he delivered heart-wrenching lines, or the passionate intensity of an actor like Sanjay Dutt, as he portrayed inner conflict and pain.

It wasn't just child's play anymore; it was preparation. His passion for films had evolved into a pursuit of mastery over emotions. Happiness, anger, sorrow - he practiced these until they felt real, until he believed he had lived them all. Each act in front of the mirror was a step closer to the destiny he hadn't yet embraced but felt destined to pursue. The power of those iconic dialogues, the strength in those performances, inspired him to mold himself into someone who could bring such depth to every role, even though the world hadn't yet seen his face on the big screen.

Born into a modest family in Mumbai, his life initially seemed far removed from the glamour of the silver screen. His formal education led him to complete a degree in hotel management - a far cry from the bright lights of showbiz. But even while managing kitchens and guest services, his heartbeat for the stage.

Determined to follow his passion, he began performing in experimental theatre productions in venues like Prithvi Theatre. A crucial mentor during this time was the legendary Marathi actor Sudhir Joshi, who encouraged him to hone his craft and pursue acting seriously.

One of his first major roles was in a play titled 'Me vs. Gandhi'. Cast as Gandhi himself, he faced a peculiar challenge - at over 100 kilograms, his physique hardly matched the image of the Mahatma. When he voiced his doubts to his mentor, Joshi teased, "Mahatma Gandhi? You? More like Frontier Gandhi!" Yet, with relentless effort, he shed the weight, embracing the role with unparalleled dedication.

Despite his talent and hard work, the road to success was anything but smooth. The film industry proved unforgiving, and rejection became a constant companion. Producers and directors often dismissed him as "talentless." With a growing family to support, he turned to his hotel management training to make ends meet.

At a Parsi hotel in Mumbai, he took a job starting from the very bottom. He worked long hours, handling laundry, room service, and occasionally earning a meagre ten-rupee tip, which felt like a small victory in those days.

One day, fate intervened. While delivering room service to a guest, he overheard a group of people in the room rehearsing film dialogues. His curiosity piqued, and he stood quietly, listening. Noticing his interest, one of them asked, "Who are you?" Nervously but honestly, he replied, "I'm a theatre actor."

To his surprise, they handed him a script and asked him to read it. Balancing the tray on his palm, he performed an impromptu reading. The room fell silent, then erupted in applause. The director offered him a role in a small film, which he accepted with unbridled enthusiasm.

The shoot lasted ten days, but just as his hopes began to

soar, he learned the film had no distributor and would never be released. The news was crushing. All that effort - wasted.

Or so he thought.

Months later, the film's rough edit landed in the hands of filmmaker Vidhu Vinod Chopra, who was fresh off the success of 'Mission Kashmir'. Impressed by the actor's performance, Chopra reached out and made an unusual proposition. "I don't have a film for you yet, but I'm booking your dates for next year," he said.

Sceptically, the actor didn't even deposit the advance cheque. It wasn't until Chopra called him again, months later, that he realised the offer was genuine. This time, he committed.

When the script arrived, he was stunned. He'd been cast in a pivotal role in a film called 'Munna Bhai MBBS'. It was his first significant role in a major production. Although he had always dreamed of being a hero, he found himself playing a strict, fatherly antagonist.

Once again, he sought advice from Sudhir Joshi. "I wanted to be a hero, not someone's father," he confessed. Joshi smiled and said, "You're an actor, not a hero. Do the role justice, and the rest will follow."

He took the advice to heart. The film became a blockbuster, and his performance as the stern yet memorable Dr. Asthana was lauded by audiences and critics alike. Overnight, he became a household name.

That little boy who once dreamt of being part of the magic of cinema had finally arrived. His journey, from a hotel room service attendant to one of the most respected actors in Indian cinema, is nothing short of extraordinary.

The actor? None other than the inimitable 'Boman Irani'.

(This story is inspired by an experience shared in "The Anupam Kher Show: Kuch bhi ho sakta hai". We do not claim any copyright or credits for it.)

Mindful Reflections: »

What is passion?

Is it something that wakes you up with excitement every morning?

Is it the driving force behind your skills and hobbies?

Or is it the unique spark that sets you apart from others?

We define passion as that inner fire that originates deep within you, propelling you to take action and bringing you happiness and contentment every day.

If you are a passionate person, chances are you are living a vibrant and fulfilling life, driven by a sense of purpose and excitement. On the other hand, if you're not aligned with your passion, life might feel monotonous, with moments of dullness creeping in, leaving you longing for something more meaningful. According to the World Health Organization (WHO), a lack of purpose and engagement in activities that bring personal fulfilment can significantly contribute to feelings of anxiety and depression. Studies indicate that approximately 40% of individuals struggle to identify their passion, while another 40% know their passion but hesitate to align their lives with it, often due to self-doubt or fear of failure.

If you find yourself in either of these categories, consider this; what if today could be the day you take the first step toward discovering your passion or trusting it enough to make it a central part of your life? The "how" is never the real obstacle; it starts with believing in your own passion and recognizing its potential to reshape your journey into one filled with purpose and joy.

As the saying goes, "Where there's a will, there's a way." When your will aligns with your passion, trust the process, take that first step, and watch how success begins to unfold. But remember, reaching a destination isn't the end - it's merely the beginning of a series of victories that define a life well-lived. Each step forward becomes another milestone, a testament to your determination and the power of your passion.

The beauty of this journey lies in the joy it brings. Passion doesn't just make the path easier; it transforms it into a fulfilling adventure. Isn't that the essence of life - to pursue what sets your soul on fire and makes every moment meaningful? Following your passion places you firmly on the throne of a truly successful life. And this will surely happen with consistency - the bridge between where you are and where you want to be.

But here's the deeper question - Are you ready to embrace this journey? Look within. What's holding you back? Is it the clarity or fear to follow your passion? The time to act is now. Trust in yourself, listen to your mind and body, take a leap, and begin the transformation today. So, pause for a moment and reflect - What will be your first step toward living a more passionate, purpose-driven life? The answer might just change or even enhance everything.

❖ ❖ ❖

"Walk as if you are kissing the Earth with
your feet." - Thích Nhất Hạnh

It is OK to be scared

In a dimly lit prison cell in China, a man sat hunched over, his hollow eyes staring at the cold, damp floor. The air was heavy with the scent of decay and despair, mirroring the weight in his chest. He was a convicted criminal, condemned to die. The gallows awaited, its shadow looming larger with each passing day. Yet, unbeknownst to him, his fate would not follow the ordinary path to death; it would take a darker, more twisted turn.

A team of doctors, fascinated by the immense and often destructive power of the human mind, had chosen him for their experiment. Their investigations into his past unearthed a chilling truth; the prisoner was utterly terrified of snakes.

The fear was not unfounded. Years ago, deep within the suffocating blackness of a coal mine, a venomous snake had slithered out of the shadows and sunk its fangs into his leg. The memory of the incident remained vivid; a sharp, burning pain that shot through his body, the frantic scramble for help, and the creeping dread as venom coursed through his veins. He had survived, but the experience had left scars that went far beyond the bite.

Since that day, snakes haunted his dreams and waking moments alike. He could still hear the rustle of scales against the coal, feel the phantom sting of venom. Even the mere mention of a snake was enough to make his pulse quicken and his hands shake uncontrollably. He avoided dark corners, damp places, and anything resembling the glint of a serpent's scales.

The doctors saw an opportunity in his fear; a key to unlock the mysteries of the mind. Determined to explore how terror could shape reality, they set their sinister plan into motion. The prisoner, with no choice but to endure, would soon find his deepest fear weaponized against him, and his mind pushed to the very brink of what it could withstand.

Every day, whispers followed him through the cold corridors.

"You will die of a snakebite."

"Any moment now, the snake will find you."

The words echoed, sharp as a hiss in the silence. Fear seeped into his bones, coiling around his thoughts like an invisible serpent. His meals tasted like dread; his steps trembled under the weight of impending doom.

One day, he approached the jailer with desperate eyes. "Kill me now," he pleaded, his voice a thin thread of despair. "Why prolong my suffering? Let me go."

The jailer said nothing, only tightened his lips and looked away.

Then came the dreaded night. The doctors told the prisoner, "Today is the day. You will face the snake."

He was led to a pitch-dark cell, the door creaking open like the entrance to a tomb. Inside, shadows danced and whispered secrets he could not decipher. As he stepped in, the door slammed shut behind him, plunging him into a suffocating void.

The room was alive. Tiny feet skittered across the floor; mice, not snakes - but in the prisoner's mind, each movement was a venomous slither. The sound of claws on stone became fangs scraping skin.

His breathing quickened. His heart thundered. The room spun as panic overwhelmed him, drowning out all reason.

Hours later, when the guards entered, they found his lifeless body curled in the corner.

The autopsy revealed the cause of death; a heart attack induced by sheer terror. But the most unsettling discovery lay in his blood. It contained traces of the very snake venom he feared, despite no snake being present.

The doctors were astounded. How could his body produce venom identical to the one from years ago? Could fear be so powerful that it rewired his biology?

The experiment had answered their question - the mind, when consumed by fear, can manifest the unimaginable.

The prisoner's tale isn't just one of death; it's a haunting reminder of the mind's untapped potential - for creation and destruction. Fear, unchecked, becomes a venom of its own, paralyzing, suffocating, and deadly.

As the story of the prisoner spread beyond the prison walls, it became a chilling parable, a testament to the power of belief, and a question that lingered in the minds of all who heard it - What fears is your own mind creating?

(This story is inspired by an anonymous source. We do not claim any copyright or credits for it.)

Mindful Reflections »

Fear, insecurity, anxiety - these emotions can strike like an unexpected storm, leaving us unsettled and overwhelmed. At their core, these feelings often stem from two patterns - worrying excessively about the future or avoiding the actions we need to take right now.

When we procrastinate on what needs our immediate attention, fear tightens its grip. It spirals into a sense of insecurity, leading to a fixed mindset where growth feels impossible. Over time, this emotional loop can erode confidence and keep us stuck mindlessly.

But there's hope. Mindfulness offers a way out, not by suppressing these emotions but by leaning into them. When fear or anxiety arises, the first step is to embrace and acknowledge it. Instead of denying how you feel or brushing it off as "just a bad day," allow yourself to sit with the emotion. Remember, emotions - especially the so-called "low-vibe" ones are messengers. They're not there to harm you but to guide you toward deeper self-awareness.

Once you've accepted the emotion, ask yourself - What is this fear trying to tell me? This simple question can be transformative. By staying with the emotion and exploring its message, you might often uncover its roots if you allow yourself to flow with this low-vibe emotion. Many times, fear is a byproduct of overthinking the future, visualizing worst-case scenarios, or using past experiences as a lens to judge the outcomes.

For example, if you feel anxious about an upcoming meeting, your fear might be rooted in a past experience where you felt judged or unprepared. Recognizing this allows you to break the cycle of assuming the same outcome and instead focus on actionable steps to prepare confidently.

Fear thrives on inaction and uncertainty. By taking even the smallest step toward addressing what you're avoiding, you shift the entire energy. Procrastination feeds insecurity, but action - no matter how small - builds resilience and confidence.

Mindfulness would always invite you to live in the present, where your empowered self truly resides. Mindfulness also always shows you a path of limitless opportunities and abundant mindset, thus setting you free from all your anxieties and fears and insecurities. By focusing on what is instead of what if, you reclaim control over your thoughts and emotions. You learn to observe fear without letting it dictate your choices.

Low-vibe emotions like fear and anxiety are not our enemies; they're signals urging you to pause, reflect, and realign. By embracing them, asking the right questions, and staying present, you can transform these emotions from barriers into bridges for growth. Eventually these low-vibe emotions would no longer haunt you because you learn not to resist them, instead you accept them and derive the necessary lessons from them.

The next time fear knocks on your door, don't run. Open it, invite it in, and listen. You might just discover the strength you didn't know you had.

❖ ❖ ❖

"The greatest battle you will ever fight is not with others but with your own mind."
— Prem Rawat

We all are judgemental, so what?

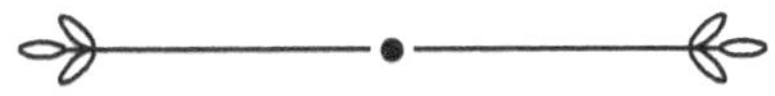

The air inside the bus was heavy with the scent of heat and diesel as Alka gripped her bag tighter, staring out the window. The lush green hills of Konkan unfolded like a painter's dream, their vibrant shades of green kissed by the sun, forming a lush, unbroken canopy. Konkan, a narrow strip of land along the western coast of India, is a treasure trove of natural beauty, where the Arabian Sea meets rugged cliffs, and endless beaches give way to dense forests. This region, known for its swaying coconut palms, mango orchards, and terraced rice fields, seemed to exist in stark contrast to the bustling chaos of Mumbai city that Alka had left behind.

As the bus rumbled along winding roads carved into hillsides, the air grew fresher, tinged with the faint aroma of salt from the distant sea. Picturesque villages with terracotta-tiled houses dotted the landscape, their red roofs peeking through thick clusters of banana and jackfruit trees. The beauty was overwhelming, almost mocking her apprehension.

Her mind swirled with thoughts of her six-year-old daughter, now staying with her mother in Mumbai. The sight of children playing under the shade of tamarind trees only heightened her longing. This assignment in Varde, an obscure village tucked deep in this verdant paradise, was a test of her resolve. Yet, as breathtaking as Konkan was, its isolation and unfamiliarity amplified her unease. The emptiness of life, it seemed, had taken yet another unexpected turn, and she wasn't sure if she was ready for it.

As the bus groaned to a stop in Malvan, Alka disembarked and was hit by the salty tang of the coastal air mixed with the earthiness of freshly churned mud. A shared jeep, cramped with locals and their wares, became her next leg of the journey. The driver hummed a rustic tune, oblivious to Alka's discomfort as she clung to the vehicle's edge. The jeep finally stopped a kilometer away from Varde. She stepped down, squinting against the sun that blazed like molten gold, and started the walk toward the village.

The road to Varde was a thin ribbon of gravel winding through coconut palms and paddy fields. The distant hum of insects filled the air, accompanied by the occasional chirp of unseen birds. As she entered the village, curious stares met her at every corner. A single woman, alone, arriving in their close-knit world; it was enough to fuel their whispers.

Alka's new home was the circuit house, a lonely bungalow with creaky floors and a fan that turned slower than the humid air. A single bed and a spartan kitchen greeted her like silent judges, their starkness echoing the isolation she already felt in this unfamiliar land. She let out a sigh, unpacked her sparse belongings, and resolved to focus on her work, convincing herself that purpose could dull the edges of discomfort.

That resolve was tested each day with the grueling commute to the substation construction site; a marathon that began before sunrise. Every morning, she trudged a kilometer to the jeep stop, boarded a rickety jeep to the train station, and then caught a train to the nearby town. The journey was as exhausting as it was relentless, leaving her spent by the time she returned each evening. Darkness cloaked the village like a heavy blanket, and fatigue clung to her like a second skin. Yet, on her very first night back, something or someone cut through her weariness. She noticed him.

The man in baggy clothes and a long beard stood at the far end of her train compartment. He was unremarkable in the crowd but somehow made her uneasy. When she alighted and took the jeep to the village's edge, she noticed him again, following her at a distance. The crunch of his footsteps on the gravel behind her felt like an echo of her growing anxiety. Her pulse quickened as she walked faster, only to hear his pace match hers. The barking of the village dogs startled her, but when she turned around, he was gone.

The pattern repeated over the next few days. The man appeared on the train, followed her to the jeep, and walked behind her toward the village. His presence became an oppressive shadow, robbing her of sleep. The village dogs offered some comfort, their growls a barrier between her and the unknown.

On the fifth day, it rained. The heavy drops drummed against her umbrella as she stepped off the jeep, but there he was again. Alka's breath hitched. The dogs were absent tonight, and she felt the emptiness like a gaping wound. She quickened her pace, but so did he. Desperation mounting, she spun around, her voice shaking as she shouted, "What's your problem? Why are you following me?"

The man stopped a few feet away, raising his hands defensively. His reply was drowned in the rain's roar. Her heart thudded as he took a step forward. She turned to run but slipped on a rock and fell, darkness overtaking her.

When Alka awoke, she was lying on a cot in an unfamiliar house. The faint aroma of spices lingered in the air. A woman with a warm smile sat beside her. "How are you feeling?" the woman asked gently.

Before Alka could answer, her eyes darted to the man standing behind the woman. Her breath caught in her throat as panic surged. "What do you want from me?" she stammered, her voice hoarse.

"Please, calm down," the woman said quickly. "This is my husband. We live in Varde too. I'm so sorry he scared you."

The man stepped forward sheepishly. "I didn't mean to frighten you," he began. "I work at the telephone office near your site. Every night, the dogs chase me. I noticed you walk fearlessly past them, and I thought... Maybe I could follow you. For protection."

Alka blinked, her fear giving way to bewilderment. "You were scared... of the dogs?" she asked, her voice tinged with incredulity.

"Yes," he admitted, scratching his head. "I didn't know how to say it without sounding foolish."

The woman chuckled softly. "We should've explained sooner. Please forgive us. Let's have dinner, and we'll walk you home."

That night, over steaming plates of rice and fish curry, Alka found herself laughing for the first time in days. The man who had seemed like a villain from an old movie turned out to be her unlikely ally. As they walked her back to the circuit house, the rain had eased into a soft drizzle, and the village felt less foreboding.

For the first time since her arrival in Varde, Alka slept soundly, comforted by the knowledge that even in the most unexpected places, kindness could be found.

Mindful Reflections: 》

We live in the present, but our past often has a way of shaping our perceptions and coloring our thoughts. It's natural to carry the memories of past experiences and interactions with us, but these memories can sometimes act as filters, distorting how we see people and situations in the present. This is where being judgmental starts; it's not a flaw but more of a reflex rooted in human nature.

If being judgmental seems to help you progress or aligns with your goals, then maybe it's not something to worry about. However, if this habit weighs you down, drains your energy, or leaves you feeling let down, or leads you to think, "Why does this always happen to me?" then perhaps it's time for some reflection.

What if you could challenge this reflex? Instead of reacting based on past assumptions, what if you could pause, step back, and view the world with fresh eyes? Mindfulness offers a way to shift from automatic judgment to intentional awareness, creating space for clarity and openness.

Here's a simple thought experiment: Think about the last time you judged someone - whether it was a colleague, a stranger in traffic, or even a friend and later realized the situation wasn't exactly what you had assumed. What triggered that judgment? Was it something they said or did? Or was it influenced by your own expectations, past experiences, or even the mood you were in that day?

Judgments often arise from the stories we tell ourselves. The key to breaking free is rewriting those stories with awareness. The next time you catch yourself judging someone, take a mindful pause. Instead of reacting immediately, ask yourself, "Is this judgment based on facts, or is it influenced by my past?" Even a few seconds of reflection can interrupt the cycle and open the door to curiosity. Judgment closes the mind, while curiosity opens it. Replace judgmental thoughts with questions like, "Why might this person be acting this way?" or "What's their story that I might not know?" Shifting from judgment to curiosity helps you understand others as complex individuals rather than reducing them to stereotypes.

Judgments tend to linger, weighing us down. Once you've paused, reflected, and gained perspective, practice letting go. Picture your judgments as leaves floating down a stream - acknowledge them, then let them drift away.

As Ellen Langer, a Harvard professor and a renowned figure in the mindfulness movement, writes in her bestselling book 'Mindfulness' - Just as mindlessness is the rigid reliance on old categories, mindfulness means the continual creation of new ones - categorizing and recategorizing, labeling and relabeling. When we make new categories in a mindful way, we pay attention to the situation and context. A mindful state also implies openness to new information. Like category making, the receiving of new information is a basic function of living creatures. Openness, noy only to new information, but to different points of view is also an important feature of mindfulness.

When we approach life with mindfulness and openness, we begin to notice shifts. Conversations become richer, relationships deepen, and our inner world grows calmer. By challenging judgments, we make room for compassion, understanding, and personal growth.

The world doesn't need us to be perfect; it just needs us to be present. So, the next time you feel a judgment rising, see it as an opportunity to pause, reflect, and become more aware. After all, isn't life more beautiful when we meet it with an open mind? Let's choose to lead with mindfulness and embrace the power of an open mind. The journey begins now.

❖ ❖ ❖

"Awareness is the greatest agent for change." - Eckhart Tolle

This is the rhythm of life

Rehan, born into the opulence of a Nawabi family in Lucknow, lived a life steeped in grandeur and tradition. His ancestral haveli, an architectural masterpiece adorned with intricate chandeliers and hand-carved jharokhas, echoed with the poetry of Mir and Ghalib, the scent of attar (also known as ittar, is a traditional natural perfume made from botanical extracts, such as flowers, herbs, and spices, distilled into a base of sandalwood oil), and the gentle strains of classical music floating through its vast courtyards. Servants in crisp white attire attended to every whim, while lavish dastarkhwans (a traditional dining space or tablecloth where food is served) overflowed with kebabs, biryanis, and aromatic shirmal, served in gleaming silver platters. Evenings were reserved for mehfils, where poets, musicians, and scholars gathered, their conversations steeped in wisdom and refinement.

Yet, behind these gilded walls, Rehan harbored a quiet rebellion. His father envisioned him as a celebrated engineer or an astute businessman, carrying forward the legacy of wealth and prestige. But Rehan found his soul in rhythm - not in the calculated world of commerce, but in the deep, resonant beats of the tabla (a pair of small hand drums used in Indian music, one of which is slightly larger than the other and is played using pressure from the heel of the hand to vary the pitch). While others admired the silk-laden tapestries of their lineage, he was drawn to the worn leather of his tabla, where every strike and vibration spoke a language beyond words. Music was his sanctuary, his secret defiance against a life dictated by duty.

His mother, being an artist at heart, came from a lineage of performers thus supported Rehan to begin his journey at the tender age of nine under the tutelage of Pandit Raghavendra, one of Lucknow's most revered tabla maestros. His training followed the ancient gurukul tradition, a way of life where students immersed themselves completely in their guru's world - not just to learn an art but to embrace its essence. For 16 years, Rehan's days began before dawn, filled with rhythmic drills, household chores for his guru, and soulful riyaz (a practice in music, dance, or art, and a name of Arabic origin) sessions under the mango trees of his guru's modest home.

But as Rehan turned 25, the allure of a different life grew stronger. By then, he had successfully completed his engineering degree, fulfilling his father's stubborn expectation. His peers showcased their modern lifestyles and global ambitions on social media, and tales of success in foreign lands sparked a longing within him. Determined to carve his own path, he set his sights on higher education at Pune University, viewing it as a gateway to his ultimate dream - moving to the United States. His father happily supported Rehan's ambitions as in his father's eyes music was a passion, not a profession.

With a heavy heart, Rehan approached his guru to share his decision. Pandit Raghavendra, seated on his worn wooden cot, listened in silence. When Rehan finished, his guru simply smiled and said, "Rhythm is a thing that lives in your heart and soul. If you want to preserve it, you must stay in touch with it or practice every day. Even if we are apart, my teachings will come to you when you truly need them."

Rehan didn't fully grasp the depth of his guru's words, his mind too enthralled by the vision of a new life awaiting him at Pune University. The promise of modern education, independence, and a future shaped by ambition dulled the weight of his parting. With a respectful bow, he touched his guru's feet, murmuring a promise to keep his music alive. Yet, as he stepped out of the familiar courtyards of Lucknow, the scent of attar lingering in the air, he couldn't shake the feeling that he was leaving behind more than just a place, he was leaving behind a part of himself.

Rehan thrived in Pune, earning accolades as an A-grade student. Soon after, he landed an opportunity to pursue his dream in Pittsburgh, USA. His life seemed picture-perfect, a prestigious job in an MNC, a beautiful home, a loving wife, and eventually, a cheerful son. Yet, as the years passed, something within Rehan began to wither. The grandeur of his Nawabi lineage in Lucknow felt like a distant memory—the sprawling courtyards, the scent of kebabs wafting through age-old havelis, the leisurely evenings filled with poetry and music under chandeliers that had seen generations of stories unfold. In contrast, his new life in the U.S. was fast-paced, efficient, and meticulously structured. Mornings were a blur of coffee on the go, traffic-laden commutes, and back-to-back meetings. The rich, unhurried traditions of Lucknow had been replaced by the digital pulse of emails and deadlines. His evenings, once filled with soulful mehfils and the deep resonance of his tabla, were now consumed by networking events, Netflix marathons, and the structured routine of American family life. Unlike the leisurely evenings of Lucknow, where conversations stretched over endless cups of chai and the air hummed with poetry and music, life in the USA was fast-paced and meticulously scheduled. Weekends were reserved for playdates, and meticulously planned outings to amusement parks or museums with his family. While he cherished the time spent with his son, helping with school projects or cheering from the sidelines at Little League games, there was an unspoken emptiness, a quiet longing for the effortless joy he once found in music. The art of savouring a moment had been traded for the efficiency of multitasking. Success was measured in promotions and paychecks, not in the depth of a raag played at dusk or the warmth of family gathered around a dastarkhwan.

With each passing year, the dissonance grew louder. He had everything he had once aspired for, yet, something felt amiss. It wasn't just nostalgia; it was the creeping realization that in chasing a future, he had abandoned a part of himself. He excelled professionally, presenting at global conferences, but a gnawing emptiness consumed him. His once-vibrant laughter faded into polite smiles. He felt like a performer in a grand play who had forgotten his lines.

One fateful day, while driving home, Rehan felt an inexplicable wave of unease. Distracted, he nearly crashed into a tree. Another day, during a high-stakes corporate presentation, he froze completely on stage, unable to utter a single word. Concerned for his well-being, his wife insisted he see a doctor. After a series of tests, the physicians found nothing physically wrong. However, sensing a deeper unrest, they recommended counseling or therapy to help him uncover the root of his growing discontent.

Rehan considered returning to India - perhaps to Pune or Lucknow - but his lifestyle in the USA felt like an unbreakable chain. His longing for purpose seemed like a distant dream.

One evening, while scrolling through his phone, Rehan stumbled upon a message in an Indian community WhatsApp group. A classical music concert was being organized that weekend, featuring renowned Indian artists. His eyes widened as he spotted Pandit Raghavendra's name among the performers. Memories of his guru and their lessons came rushing back, filling him with a long-lost excitement.

That week, Rehan's wife noticed a change in him. He was energetic, humming tunes, and smiling more often. She thought perhaps therapy was finally working.

On the day of the concert, Rehan arrived at the venue an hour early, eager to meet his guru after 15 years. He made his way backstage and found himself face-to-face with

Pandit Raghavendra. The guru's hair had turned silver, but his aura remained as commanding as ever.

"Rehan!" the guru exclaimed with warmth.

Overwhelmed, Rehan fell at his guru's feet, tears streaming down his face. "Guruji, I've lost myself. I feel like a failure, even with all my success."

Pandit Raghavendra placed a comforting hand on his shoulder and said, "You haven't lost yourself, Rehan. You might have simply lost touch with your rhythm."

As the concert began, Pandit Raghavendra did something unexpected. He held Rehan's hand and led him onto the stage. Rehan hesitated, embarrassed that he hadn't touched a tabla in over a decade. But his guru smiled reassuringly and announced to the audience, "Today, I have a special guest with me - my student Rehan, who I met here after 15 years. With your permission, I'd like him to play alongside me."

Rehan's heart pounded as he sat before the tabla, a whirlwind of doubt clouding his mind. His fingers trembled above the drumheads, uncertain, hesitant. But then, as if guided by an unseen force, they struck the surface - and in that instant, something magical happened. The rhythm poured out effortlessly, each beat resonating with a deep familiarity, as though his hands had never abandoned their craft. It was a stark contrast to the conference stage where he had meticulously prepared, only to freeze under the weight of expectation. Here, after 15 years of absence, the music surged through him instinctively, unrestrained and pure. The audience sat spellbound, but more than that, Rehan himself was captivated - by the undeniable truth that this, this rhythm, had always been a part of him, waiting to be rediscovered.

At that moment, he understood his guru's words from years ago. Rhythm wasn't just a skill; it was a connection to his soul. The tabla became his voice, the music his language. For the first time in years, Rehan felt whole. Rehan realized that while he couldn't change the past, he could bring music back into his life. Over the next few months, Rehan began integrating tabla practice into his daily routine. He even started teaching his son, passing down the wisdom of his guru. Though he stayed in the USA, he reconnected with his roots, blending his Nawabi heritage with his modern life. Rehan's journey wasn't about choosing between two worlds; it was about finding his rhythm in both.

Mindful Reflections: 》

Life is a continuous flow, a dance of moments, actions, emotions, and experiences, all coming together in a beautifully complex rhythm. Just like the beats of a song, life's rhythm can guide us, energize us, and at times, even challenge us.

When I mention rhythm, what's the first thing that comes to your mind?

Is it a drumbeat, a dance movement, or perhaps your favorite song?

Yes, to all of the above - because rhythm is about flow, about movement, about grooving through life.

So let me ask you - What keeps you moving and grooving? If not now, then maybe a few years ago - what was it that pushed you to take bold steps or make important decisions?

This is exactly what we are here to explore.

Passion is often either glorified or underestimated. But what if we viewed passion as something as natural as breathing? Without breath, we wouldn't be alive, right? The same goes for passion - it is the invisible force, the rhythm of our lives. It isn't something external that we need to search for; it already exists within us. Sometimes, we lose touch with it, but as long as we're alive, it never truly disappears.

Passion fuels rhythm in a way that transforms ordinary moments into extraordinary experiences. Imagine a dancer moving effortlessly to a beat - the rhythm is in their body, guiding them - but it's their passion for the dance that makes each movement come alive. Similarly, when we discover something that excites us, whether it's a project, a relationship, or a creative pursuit, it becomes the rhythm that drives our lives. This rhythm isn't just routine; it's infused with life, energy, and purpose. It is the heartbeat that urges us forward, keeping us connected to what truly matters to us.

Yet, in the rush of daily life, many of us lose connection with this rhythm. We get caught up in routines, responsibilities, and expectations. We move mechanically, forgetting the passion that once lit up our path. Life becomes a monotonous loop - a rhythm without soul.

When this happens, we might just need to take a pause and reflect.

Rhythm isn't just about repetition - it's about alignment. It's about finding joy in what we do. Passion isn't a one-time event; it's a pulse that runs through everyday life. Even in the most ordinary moments, passion can be rekindled if we take the time to tune in. Whether you're experiencing a moment of joy or surfing through a difficult phase, the rhythm of life is always there – waiting to be noticed. The secret is to let passion shape this rhythm, transforming it from something mundane into something meaningful. Just like a dancer adjusts to changes in tempo, we too can learn to move with life's shifting beats. The rhythm doesn't have to be perfect, it just has to be yours.

So, what makes your heart race?

What ignites that spark in you?

What absorbs you so completely that time seems to stand still?

When you find that, you've found your rhythm. And with it, you've found your passion.

In the end, life's rhythm is the soundtrack to your journey. The tempo will change, the beat may slow down or speed up, but what truly matters is how you move with it. Passion is what turns every step into a dance. So, release the pressure to follow someone else's beat. Instead, tune into your own. This is your rhythm. This is your life. And when you live it with passion, you'll discover that the dance never really ends.

"Every breath is a fresh start"
- Shweta Kulkarni

Your reality is what YOU believe

Dr. Ravi had been asthmatic since birth. Diagnosed with asthma in his childhood, he always carried his blowpipe, a constant companion that allowed him to breathe normally. Doctors had assured him that as he grew older, the condition would subside. Ravi, however, was never drawn to sports, which left him free to focus on his studies and excel academically.

But one day, during his school's annual function, Ravi's world was shaken. As he carried a bouquet of roses to welcome guests on stage, disaster struck. His breath caught in his chest, and before he knew it, he collapsed. The school rushed him to the hospital, and though he recovered, doctors advised him to stay far away from roses, suggesting they were the trigger for his asthma.

Ravi, despite his health challenges, became a top student, excelling in his 10th grade and deciding to pursue a career in medicine. However, his asthma seemed to worsen over time, and the blowpipe became more and more necessary. Determined to find answers, he studied gynaecology but continued to seek the counsel of asthma specialists, who failed to diagnose his condition.

It was during his years in medical college that Ravi met a girl. She was smart, caring, and beautiful. One day, as they spoke in the college courtyard, she confessed that she liked him and wanted to take their relationship seriously. As she extended her hand, a red rose appeared in her grasp. The sight of the flower sent Ravi into a panic, and before he could react, he fainted on the spot. The girl, terrified and confused, never spoke to him again.

Despite his medical career taking off - he became a successful gynaecologist, Ravi's condition remained a constant battle. His career often clashed with his health; he would avoid rooms filled with flowers and would never stay in the presence of roses, fearing an asthma attack. Once, after successfully delivering a healthy baby, Ravi was unable to enter the room to check on the mother, as it was filled with flower bouquets. The situation was frustrating, and Ravi felt trapped by his own body.

But one day, fate led him to Dr. Swami, a renowned pulmonary expert, at a medical conference in the USA. Dr. Swami's speech was captivating, and Ravi, desperate for answers, reached out to him. Despite Dr. Swami's busy schedule, he agreed to see Ravi for a brief 10-minute consultation a week later. Ravi was instructed to send his medical history, and he was adamant about one thing - no flowers, no roses.

When the day came, Ravi arrived at Dr. Swami's hospital in Bangalore, but the moment he stepped out of his car, panic set in. The nurse welcoming him wore a red rose in her hair. The ward boy had a rose pinned to his shirt. As Ravi made his way into the building, he noticed that the elevator was wallpapered with roses. His heart raced, and his anxiety shot through the roof. He tried to take the stairs, but even they were lined with roses. His breath caught in his chest, and he collapsed in the hallway, succumbing to a severe asthma attack.

When Ravi regained consciousness, he found himself in Dr. Swami's office. Furious and confused, he demanded answers. "I'm going to sue you! You've deliberately put me in danger! I told you about my condition - why did you do this?" he shouted.

Dr. Swami, calm as ever, smiled. "I understand your frustration, Ravi. But nothing happened to you. You're perfectly fine."

Before Ravi could respond, Dr. Swami pulled out a red rose and held it out to him. "Touch it," he said.

Ravi hesitated, bewildered. He took the rose, his mind racing. But then something remarkable happened. The rose was fake, made of plastic!

Dr. Swami chuckled softly. "None of the roses you saw today were real. Your asthma isn't caused by flowers, Ravi. It's your fear and anxiety about them that triggers your condition. Your mind believes that roses are dangerous, and that belief has kept you trapped. If you let go of that belief, your asthma will disappear."

Ravi's mind began to calm. He stared at the rose in his hand, the realization dawning on him. All his years of suffering, all his anxiety about flowers, had been based on a false belief. For the first time in his life, he felt free.

Later that day, as he left Dr. Swami's clinic, Ravi placed the fake rose on the desk in the check-up room, along with a note that read: "Thank you, Doctor. I leave my beliefs here today." As he walked out into the sunlight, a sense of peace settled over him. He had let go of the fear that had defined his life for so long. And for the first time, he breathed freely, unburdened by the past.

(This story is inspired by an anonymous source. We do not claim any copyright or credits for it.)

Mindful Reflections: ⟫

What Is Reality? Yours, Mine, or Something Universal?

Reality is often defined as "the state of things as they actually exist, as opposed to an idealistic or notional idea of them." But if reality were purely objective, why do different people perceive the same situation in entirely different ways?

The truth is, reality is not just about what exists – it's about what we believe exists. It is shaped by our past experiences, belief systems, and personal values.

Take this example, you have 75 lakhs in your bank account. How do you see it? One person might say, "I'm 25 lakhs short of a crore." Another might think, "I have almost a crore!" The numbers don't change, but the perception does.

Now, imagine an eighth-grader who is constantly told, "You're weak in math." No matter how hard he studies, he carries this belief like a weight. His fear of failure reinforces his struggle, and despite his best efforts, he may continue to fall short, not because he isn't capable, but because he believes he isn't.

This happens to all of us. We unconsciously absorb the labels and narratives assigned to us - whether by parents, teachers, friends, or colleagues. If we lack self-awareness and self-confidence we let the world define our reality for us. We start believing statements like, "You're not good enough." "You can't do this." "You can never be financially independent." And so, we live within these invisible boundaries, forgetting that we have the power to change the script.

Could you pause for a moment and reflect;

What reality do you want in your relationships?

What reality do you want in your career and finances?

What reality do you want when people think of you as a person?

If you don't take control of your reality, someone else will, whether it's society, past experiences, or the opinions of others. The world will always have a version of who you should be. But the real question is - Do you accept that version, or do you create your own?

To truly shape your reality, you must challenge the beliefs that have silently dictated your life. The doubts, the fears, the self-imposed limitations - most of them exist only in your mind. They are stories you have been told, narratives you've internalized. But they are not absolute truths.

What if, instead of viewing yourself through the lens of past failures, you redefined yourself by your potential? What if you released the weight of old fears and embraced the boundless possibilities of what could be?

Your mind is a powerful architect, shaping the world you

experience. Every thought you nurture, every belief you reinforce, becomes the foundation of your reality. So why not build one that empowers you? Right now, at this very moment, you have the power to choose.

What reality do you want to create?

What do you see for yourself in your relationships, career, health, and self-image?

Don't just think about it - write it down. Let your thoughts take shape on paper, turning them from fleeting ideas into intentions with purpose. Your reality is yours to shape. The only question is - How will you start designing the life you truly want?

❖ ❖ ❖

"The mind is everything. What you think,
you become." - Buddha

Great Responsibility reveals Great Power

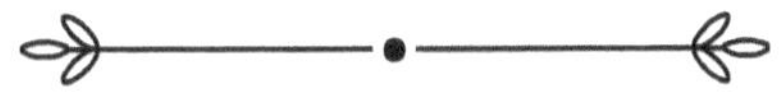

In the heart of Mumbai - a city of towering apartments, bustling streets, and relentless ambition - lived a young man of about 25. Nobody knew where he came from or how long he had been there, yet he was as much a part of the society as the honking rickshaws and the distant roar of the local trains.

They called him Addha, meaning "half." Half a man, half understood, half noticed. Too short for his age, a little slow to comprehend things, but ever-present. He didn't belong to anyone, yet everyone claimed a part of him.

Mumbai, the city of dreams, rarely had space for a pause. Every inch of land was occupied, every breath intertwined with a million others. The city did not have sprawling houses with gardens; instead, it had apartments stacked like matchboxes, where lives overlapped, secrets were thin walls apart, and space was a luxury few could afford. Yet, in this concrete jungle, Mumbai had a way of embracing all, villagers arriving with nothing but hope, dreamers seeking fortune, outcasts looking for a second chance. It didn't ask for backgrounds or surnames. If you could survive its chaos, you belonged.

And in this vast, indifferent city, Addha belonged.

If the fourth-floor aunty needed vegetables, she'd call Addha. The first-floor uncle, who couldn't be seen buying cigarettes himself, relied on Addha. The kids needed an extra player for cricket? Addha stepped in. A wedding in society? Addha ran errands. He never asked for money, never complained, never refused. The old watchman, whose tiny security cabin stood at the gate, let Addha sleep there at night. No one knew how long he had been around. He was just… there as a silent helper. His presence was constant, yet sadly his absence wouldn't be noticed, until someone needed something.

One evening, a vibrant wedding procession passed by the society. The blaring band music and swirling lights drew everyone to their balconies. Suddenly, someone pointed out, "Look, Addha is dancing!" Laughter echoed as the residents mocked him, but Addha didn't care. He danced with abandon, immersing himself in a joy he seldom experienced.

But his carefree life shifted the day Reena, a college student from the 6th floor, was harassed by a group of bullies. Scared and desperate, she called out to Addha, who was walking by with a laundry bag. Without hesitation, Addha ran to her, held her hand, and escorted her home. She thanked him warmly, calling him sweet, and walked away.

For the first time, Addha felt something stir within him, an emotion he didn't quite understand. He began dressing differently, donning an old pair of jeans and a stitched-up colorful shirt. He waited for Reena outside her college, eager to help with her books and bags. But one day, he overheard her laughing with her boyfriend. "What? Him? That Addha? He's half in every way - half a mind, half a man!" They both laughed, their words cutting deeper than Addha ever thought possible.

That night, Addha sat with the watchman, drowning his sorrow in cheap whiskey. The rejection stung, but it opened his eyes. He realized he was nothing more than a convenience to society. From that day, Addha changed. He started charging for his work, shocking everyone.

Around this time, a new resident moved into a vacant flat on the 5th floor. Satya was a well-dressed, enigmatic woman who lived alone. Gossip spread quickly, she was an escort, people said. Men visited her discreetly, yet they were the loudest in spreading rumors. The society turned hostile toward Satya, but her connections kept her safe.

Few years passed, and life went on. Reena married her boyfriend and moved away. Addha watched her wedding from a distance, the pain of unspoken emotions weighing heavily on him. That night, he climbed to the terrace with a bottle of whiskey. He was lost in thought when Satya appeared. She silently sat beside him, taking a sip from his bottle. No words were exchanged, but their shared loneliness was palpable.

The next day, Addha vanished. No one knew where he went, and no one cared enough to find out. His absence was felt only when chores piled up.

Months later, Satya's health deteriorated. The society's cold judgment, the stress, the loneliness - it all took its toll. She gave birth to a baby girl, but her body couldn't handle it. One morning, Satya died in her apartment.

The baby lay beside her, crying. The society gathered, murmuring, whispering, but nobody stepped forward. They called the authorities, discussed what to do with the child, but no one wanted to take responsibility.

Then, someone noticed a familiar figure pushing through the crowd.

"Addha?"

He was back. Quietly, without a word, he walked past the gossiping voices, stepped into Satya's apartment, and looked at her one last time. Then, he picked up the baby girl and turned away.

As he walked out of the society gates, the watchman muttered under his breath, "The incomplete ones are these people. Addha is the responsible one - the complete man."

From that day on, Addha was never seen in the society again. But his act of quiet bravery left an indelible mark. To the world, he had been "half," but in that moment, he proved he was more whole than anyone could ever be.

(This story is inspired by the works of writer Gulzar. We do not claim any copyright or credits for it.)

Mindful Reflections: 》

Imagine a world where each of us plays our role with the utmost proficiency, giving our best in every moment. What a remarkable place it would be! Responsibility is not

not in what we are called but in what we choose to do.

If the thought crosses your mind – why should I take all the responsibility? – perhaps the concept has been misunderstood. As individuals, we can only control what is within our reach. Just as mindfulness teaches us to be aware of only the present moment, let us focus solely on our own actions. Naturally, we will act in ways that align with our values and beliefs. For example, if I see someone littering in a public space, my instinctive response is to ask them to dispose of their trash properly. If a child begs at a traffic signal, I feel compelled to encourage them to seek education or earn a living with dignity instead of falling into the cycle of begging.

So, if you were to take responsibility for something, what would it be? Would you act without needing to be asked? Would the courage to take responsible action flow naturally within you? Because only great responsibility generates greater power. We have just one life – let us make the most of it. Do your best, whenever and however you can, so that you never look back with regret, thinking, I wish I had taken action when I had the chance.

"We are all born with unique gifts; the key
is to focus on developing those talents."
- Robert Greene

Episode 21

Are you aware every time you get angry?

Balarama, Sri Krishna, and Satyaki were legendary figures from ancient Indian epics. Balarama, the elder brother of Krishna, was known for his immense strength and skill with the plow, often depicted as a symbol of duty and discipline. Sri Krishna, revered as an incarnation of Lord Vishnu, was wise, strategic, and known for his divine charm and ability to guide others with profound teachings. Satyaki, a fearless warrior and a devoted disciple of Krishna, was known for his loyalty and unmatched bravery in battle.

These three warriors were on an important mission, tasked with delivering a crucial message to a neighboring kingdom. Taking a shortcut through the dense forest, they hoped to reach their destination swiftly. The sun hung low in the sky, casting long shadows as Balarama, Sri Krishna, and Satyaki rode through the dense forest. Their horses, swift as the wind, had carried them far from the comforts of their palace. Now, as twilight melted into darkness, an uneasy silence blanketed the woods. The rustling of leaves and distant calls of nocturnal creatures set an ominous tone.

"We should halt here for the night," Balarama suggested, dismounting his horse. The others nodded in agreement. They tethered their steeds to sturdy trees and gathered around a small clearing. A cool breeze whispered through the branches, but it carried a supernatural stillness that made the hairs on the back of Satyaki's neck rise.

"We must take turns standing guard," Krishna proposed. "Each of us will watch over the camp for a quarter of the night while the others rest." The others nodded in agreement, understanding the need for caution in the unfamiliar forest.

Satyaki took the first watch. He sat upright, alert, his ears straining to catch any unusual sound. Suddenly, a harsh roar shattered the quiet. Emerging from the darkness was a towering figure - a freakish specter with hollow, fiery eyes and a body that seemed to shift and grow with each passing second.

The ghost bared its jagged teeth. "Leave now, and I shall spare you. But if you permit me to devour the other two, I will do you no harm."

For a fleeting moment, fear gripped Satyaki, but his warrior spirit refused to succumb. Determined to protect his companions, he steadied himself, his blood boiling with resolve. Rising to his feet, he fixed his gaze on the monstrous figure and bellowed, "You wretched creature! Do you think I fear you? If you value your life, vanish this instant, or I will crush you where you stand!"

The ghost let out another roar, its form swelling, muscles

rippling like storm clouds. It attacked Satyaki, who met it with fierce determination. They wrestled, their struggle kicking up dirt and leaves. The beast hurled Satyaki to the ground, its strength growing with every angry cry. Satyaki fought courageously but was battered and bruised. His limbs ached, his breaths came in ragged gasps, and just as he thought he could take no more, the night's first quarter ended - and the ghost suddenly vanished.

Exhausted, Satyaki shook Balarama awake. "Your turn," he muttered, sinking into the forest floor.

Balarama, strong and fearless, stood his ground. No sooner had the exhausted Satyaki slipped into unconsciousness than the ghost reappeared, its menacing form looming once more.

"Surrender your companions, and I shall spare you," it sneered.

Balarama, too, was struck by the ghostly presence, yet he fearlessly clenched his fists. "I did sooner break every bone in my body than heed the words of a vile creature like you!"

With a battle cry and sense of responsibility given by Sri Krishna, he lunged at the ghost. The fight was more brutal - blows landed like thunderclaps, and the very earth trembled beneath them. Yet, just like before, the more Balarama's fury grew, the larger and more monstrous the ghost became. They struggled, locked in a violent dance until the second quarter of the night ended. As suddenly as it had come, the specter vanished into the void.

Drenched in sweat, Balarama panted as he shook Krishna awake. "Beware," he warned. "A supernatural beast is lurking, waiting to devour us!"

Krishna sat cross-legged in the clearing, his face serene as the moon above. When the ghost returned, its eyes gleamed with malice.

"Run while you can, and leave these two behind," it hissed.

Krishna chuckled. "Oh, how kind of you to visit! I was beginning to feel lonely. Why don't you stay? We could keep each other company until dawn."

The ghost, taken aback, growled and lunged at him. But unlike the others, Krishna neither fought nor resisted. Instead, he smiled and said, "Ah, such vigor! You must be quite proud of your strength."

The ghost hesitated, its form flickering.

"You are indeed a mighty fighter! Such boundless energy!" Krishna added, his voice laced with amusement.

The specter trembled. Its body, once enormous, began to shrink. It flailed, trying to feed off Krishna's anger - but there was none. With each word, its strength diminished until it was no larger than a worm. Krishna picked it up and tied it into the corner of his blanket, chuckling softly.

At dawn, Balarama and Satyaki awoke. They stretched, groaning at their bruises. Krishna, ever composed, watched them with a knowing smile.

"What happened to you two?" he asked innocently.

They recounted their terrifying encounters, the fierce battles, the overwhelming strength of the ghost.

Krishna laughed and opened his blanket, revealing the tiny, squirming worm. "This is your fearsome ghost," he said, placing it on the ground.

Balarama and Satyaki stood frozen in awe and disbelief.

Krishna continued, "Anger is like this creature. The more you feed it, the bigger it grows. But if you remain calm, it shrinks into nothingness. Remember, controlling your own anger weakens the anger of others."

As his words settled, the ghostly presence faded into the morning mist, dissolving like a shadow before the rising sun. The golden light filtered through the dense canopy, illuminating the forest with a quiet serenity. Balarama and Satyaki exchanged glances, their hearts still pounding but their minds now clear. The truth was undeniable - true strength was not in the force of their fists but in the mastery of their emotions. With a newfound understanding, they followed Krishna, their steps lighter, leaving behind not just the ghost, but the weight of their own unchecked fury.

(This story is inspired by an anonymous source. We do not claim any copyright or credits for it.)

Mindful reflections: ⟫

Anger is one of the most misunderstood emotions. We often might hear statements like, "People who are not angry are good people," implying that anger is a flaw. But is it really? Anger is simply an emotion - one that every human being experiences. The difference lies in how we express it. Some people react outwardly, raising their voices or confronting the source of their frustration, while others turn inward, shutting down or suppressing their feelings behind a composed exterior. Neither response makes someone inherently 'angry' or good.' What truly matters is how we understand, then process and drive this powerful emotion.

Imagine a scenario - Someone stole something from you

on a Monday which made you angry on Tuesday. On Wednesday that person returned what he stole. Now, that someone compensates you for any disadvantage occasioned to you for not having had that thing for two days; offers additional gifts to show the good will; apologizes for the theft as a moment of weakness; and finally, promises never to do it again. Could it be rational for you to be just as angry on Thursday as you were on Tuesday? Moreover, could it be rational for you to conceive of a plan to steal from that person in turn? Pheww! you might want to read it again. It is very human for us to be angry. We just need to remember that anger is a low vibe emotion and it is necessary to embrace it.

This example highlights how anger can outlast the situation that triggered it, feeding on our own thoughts rather than the actual event. Anger, like any other emotion, serves a purpose – it signals that something needs attention. However, when left unchecked, it can spiral into prolonged suffering, clouding our judgment and harming our overall well-being.

In our above story, Lord Shri Krishna, who offers profound wisdom on dealing with anger, teaches that anger is much like a monstrous entity, grows when fed and diminishes when ignored. The more we dwell on our grievances, the stronger our anger becomes. But if we choose to remain calm and observe it without reacting, it gradually loses its grip on us.

One of the core principles of mindfulness is awareness – being conscious of our emotions without letting them control us. When anger arises, rather than suppressing it or letting it explode, mindfulness invites us to pause and acknowledge it. Ask yourself – Why am I feeling angry? Is it because whatever happened did not fit into my values and beliefs? Is it because I am not taking action in alignment with my heart and mind? These reflections shift our focus from the external trigger to our internal state, helping us address the root cause rather than merely reacting to the surface-level issue.

Acceptance is the first step in managing anger mindfully. Instead of resisting the emotion, recognize that you are angry because an unwanted or unpleasant situation has occurred. Once you accept this, the next step is choosing how to respond. Can you change the situation? If not, how can you shift your perspective to deal with it in a healthier way?

In the concluding part of the above story, Lord Krishna emphasizes that true strength lies not in suppressing anger but in mastering it. Just as the morning sun dispels the darkness, awareness and wisdom can dissolve the hold of anger over us. Krishna's lesson is clear – By accepting our own anger, we weaken the anger of others because there is no resistance left within us.

To wrap up this reflection, I invite you to engage in a mindful activity – forgiving yourself for any suffering your anger may have caused you. Anger often lingers because we attach guilt, shame, or frustration to it. Instead, practice self-compassion. Acknowledge that anger is a natural emotion, but suffering is optional. By embracing awareness and mindfulness, you can transform anger from a consuming fire into a source of growth and self-reflection. Remember, all emotions naturally arise in response to our circumstances and influences. Mindfulness encourages us to accept every emotion, ask ourselves why we feel a certain way, and trust that the answers will emerge, guiding us toward the next right action.

Hey, remember this – YOU ARE RESOURCEFUL!

*"Be happy in the moment, that's enough.
Each moment is all we need, not more."*
- Mother Teresa

Only knowledge would set you free

In the small village of Naigaon, Maharashtra, a girl was born who would one day defy centuries of oppression and transform the landscape of education in India. Savitribai Phule, with an innate curiosity and strong ambition, was destined for a path few dared to tread. At the tender age of nine, she was married to Jyotirao Phule, a young man who would later become not just her husband but her greatest ally in a revolution for women's education and social justice.

Savitribai's thirst for knowledge was evident from a young age. One day, she was caught tearing pages from an English-language book, an object forbidden to girls of her caste and status. Her father, outraged, snatched the book from her hands and hurled it away, commanding her never to touch one again. In that moment, instead of submission, a spark ignited in Savitribai - she vowed to learn to read and write, no matter the obstacles. Her most treasured possession soon became a book gifted by a

Christian missionary, a symbol of the education she so fiercely desired.

Her journey began under the shade of a mango tree, where Jyotirao broke a twig into two, shaping them into makeshift pens. Handing them to Savitribai and his aunt Sagunabai, he instructed them to carve an alphabet into the soil. Little did they know that this simple act would lay the foundation for women's education in India. The first letter she traced was more than just an alphabet - it was history in the making.

Recognizing her passion, Jyotirao took it upon himself to teach her. At a time when Pune was a stronghold of rigid Brahmanical traditions, education for lower-caste women was unthinkable. Yet, Savitribai persisted. In 1840, she and Sagunabai enrolled in the Normal School established by Mrs. Michelle, a British woman. There, she read about Thomas Clarkson, a British anti-slavery activist, and was struck by the parallels between the struggles of African slaves and the oppression faced by Dalits and women in India. Education, she realized, was the only weapon powerful enough to break these chains.

Determined to formalize her learning, Savitribai undertook teacher training in Ahmednagar and Pune, becoming a qualified teacher by 1847. Her success, however, was met with resistance. Each day, on her way to school, she was pelted with stones and cowdung by those who opposed her mission. Unfazed, she carried an extra saree, changing her clothes upon arrival before stepping into her classroom with dignity and resolve.

By 1848, she and Jyotirao took a bold step - establishing India's first school for girls in Pune. The move sent shockwaves through society. The idea of women receiving education was met with such outrage that they were forced to leave their own home in 1849, disowned by their families for defying the Manusmriti's rigid caste and gender norms. Yet, they remained undeterred, opening more schools, including one in a Dalit settlement where no teacher dared to work. When no one else would, Savitribai and Sagunabai taught the students themselves.

Education transformed the lives of their students. Two young girls, Muktabai Mang and Tarabai Shinde, became pioneers in feminist literature, their writings on caste and gender oppression remaining relevant to this day. Even British officials took note. Major Candy of Pune University remarked on the intelligence and sincerity of the students, acknowledging that their curriculum was on par with the best in the country.

Beyond education, Savitribai was a force for social reform. In 1853, she and Jyotirao established an education society, opening 18 schools for girls across Maharashtra. They founded Balhatya Pratibandhak Griha, a shelter for rape victims and pregnant women excluded by society. In 1854, she opened a home for widows, ensuring they received an education and the dignity they were so often denied. She even adopted Yashwantrao, the child of a widow in her shelter, breaking yet another societal norm.

In 1868, the Phules challenged another deep-seated injustice - access to water. In a society where untouchables were forbidden from drawing water from common wells, they dug their own well in their backyard, ensuring that no one in their community would go thirsty. The act was revolutionary, sending tremors through a caste-driven society.

Savitribai also played a key role in shaping the Satyashodhak Samaj (The Truthseekers' Society), founded by Jyotirao to promote equality and reject caste-based discrimination. In 1873, she pioneered the concept of Satyashodhak Marriage, where couples pledged to uphold education and equality instead of adhering to oppressive religious customs.

Her contributions did not go unnoticed. In 1852, the British government declared her the best teacher in the state, and in 1853, she was commended once again for her groundbreaking work in education. However, her most defiant act came in 1890 when, upon Jyotirao's death, she broke all societal norms by lighting his funeral pyre herself - an act traditionally reserved for men.

Even after her husband's passing, she carried forward his mission, taking charge of the Satyashodhak Samaj and continuing to fight for the marginalized. Today, Pune University, known as the 'Oxford of the East,' bears her name - a tribute to her extraordinary contribution to education and social reform.

Had Savitribai Phule yielded to the obstacles before her, would India have seen the light of female education and social emancipation? Her story is not just one of struggle, but of triumph - a testament to the transformative power of knowledge. She understood that education was the key to progress, a lesson that remains just as relevant today. If we can embody even a fraction of her resilience, no force in the world can hinder our journey toward true progress. For in learning, we find liberation, and in education, we find the power to change the world.

Mindful Reflections: »

Have you ever wondered what the most valuable source of power in your life is? Something that no one can ever take away from you? Is it money? Your house? Your car? Your relationships?

Think deeper.

It is knowledge - the wisdom, skills, and learning you accumulate over time.

Knowledge is the most powerful asset you can possess. It has the ability to transform lives, break barriers, and even shape the future. Unlike material possessions, which can be lost, stolen, or devalued, knowledge remains with you, empowering you every step of the way.

At any stage of life, never limit yourself. Never stop learning. Growth isn't confined to a classroom or a particular age - it's a lifelong journey. Whether it's enhancing your current skills, advancing in your career, or diving into an entirely new field that could lead to financial independence, every bit of learning adds immense value to both your personal and professional life.

If you have a job or business, ask yourself - are you truly tapping into your full potential? If the answer is no, it's time to take action. Learn a new skill. Explore a secondary income stream. Often, we overlook the fact that many of our hobbies have the potential to be monetized. Why not refine those natural talents and turn them into opportunities? Upskill, experiment, and see where it takes you.

Let me say it again - never stop learning.

Knowledge grants you freedom, with freedom comes creativity, and, most importantly, wisdom. A society that prioritizes education experiences real progress, development, and transformation. This was the very belief that drove Smt. Savitribai Phule and her husband, Jyotiba Phule, two of India's most legendary education reformers. At a time when education was denied to women and marginalized communities, they stood by their conviction that knowledge is the key to social reformation. Their relentless efforts paved the way for countless individuals to access education and build a better future.

Now, let's turn the spotlight on you. Take a moment to reflect;

What skills have you always wanted to learn?

Are there certifications or courses you've been postponing?

Is there a degree you always wished to pursue?

Make a list. Prioritize them. Because investing in knowledge is investing in yourself. And that is an investment that will always yield maximum returns.

❖ ❖ ❖

"Truth can be stated in a thousand different ways, yet each one can be true." - Swami Vivekananda

Change is
the only constant

The year was 1986. The bustling streets of Mumbai hummed with life, rickshaws honking, vendors shouting their wares, the scent of fresh samosas mingling with the aroma of brewing chai. Amidst the chaos, two twin brothers, Prakash and Subhash, stood at the crossroads of their lives. They had always been inseparable - identical in appearance, yet starkly different in nature.

Prakash, the elder by a few minutes, was assertive, sharp-tongued, and driven. Subhash, on the other hand, was quiet, thoughtful, and often a step behind his brother. As children, they played pranks on unsuspecting neighbors, their identical faces causing endless confusion. But childhood mischief had given way to adult responsibilities, and now, they both had families to support.

One evening, as they sat on the terrace of their shared home, Prakash leaned forward excitedly. "I have an idea,

Subhash. A phone booth! Everyone needs to make calls, but who has a telephone at home? If we open one, people will line up outside."

Subhash nodded, intrigued. He had always followed Prakash's lead, and this time was no different. Within months, both brothers had their own telephone booths, barely a hundred meters apart. Bright yellow boxes stood proudly on the street, their constant ringing merging with the city's endless noise. Business boomed. The queues never ended. People traveled from far to use their services, and in no time, the brothers were making more money than they had ever imagined.

For ten years, life was smooth. They thrived together, growing prosperous, their families sharing dinners, laughter, and dreams. Until one morning in 1995, when Subhash's eyes fell on a newspaper headline.

"Mobile phones launched in India."

His hands trembled as he read on. A device that allows you to talk while walking, traveling, or even sitting at home? It sounded unbelievable, yet it was already happening in America and Europe. Subhash felt a chill run down his spine. If this technology took over, what would happen to their booths?

That night, he paced around his room before finally approaching Prakash. "Bhai, we need to think ahead. Mobile phones are coming. If people start buying them, who will use our booths?"

Prakash scoffed, waving him off. "You worry too much. Do you think people will abandon an eighty-year-old system overnight? Even the British still use telephone booths! Forget this nonsense."

Subhash hesitated but felt an unshakable pull towards the future. His wife listened patiently as he shared his concerns. "If this change is inevitable, we should be ready," she said. Her words gave him courage. He spent weeks researching and finally made a decision - he would open a mobile phone store.

When he shared his plan with Prakash, his brother laughed. "You'll lose everything, Subhash! Don't come crying to me when your foolish idea fails."

Undeterred, Subhash took out a loan and set up a small mobile shop next to his telephone booth. At first, customers came only out of curiosity. "It's too expensive," they would mutter before walking away.

Days turned into weeks, and still, sales were dismal. Meanwhile, Prakash never missed a chance to taunt him.

"I told you, didn't I? You've lost your mind! Look at me - I'm still making money while you're wasting your time."

Doubt gnawed at Subhash. Had he made a mistake? Would his decision cost his family everything? The burden of his loan felt heavier each day. The once-close brothers grew distant, their interactions limited to curt nods and silent meals.

Then, as the new millennium dawned, something changed. Mobile phone prices dropped. More brands entered the market. Suddenly, people weren't just curious, they wanted to buy. Subhash's shop, which once stood empty, now had a queue stretching down the road. His single shop turned into three. He sold SIM cards, accessories, and repairs.

One day, Prakash walked into the store, his eyes scanning the bustling crowd. He saw the excitement, the exchanges of crisp rupee notes, the beaming faces of customers walking away with their first mobile phones. He saw success-his brother's success.

Subhash spotted him and smiled. "Would you like some tea, brother?"

They sat outside, the familiar clinking of tea glasses between them. Prakash stirred his tea absently, lost in thought. After a long silence, he finally spoke. "I used to think you lacked wisdom, but you proved me wrong and changed everything."

Subhash took a sip of his tea and replied, "Time changed, brother. And with time, we must change too. You haven't lost to me, you lost to time."

Prakash exhaled deeply, his pride crumbling. He looked at his brother - the same brother he had laughed at, doubted, and dismissed. And yet, here they were, with the tables turned.

He smiled, a bittersweet smile, and reached over to hug his brother. The city moved around them, the honking rickshaws, the street vendors, the endless chatter of people. But in that moment, amidst the noise, a silent understanding passed between them.

Change was inevitable. And for the first time, Prakash embraced it.

Mindful Reflections: »

We humans are wired for happiness, and one of the greatest sources of joy is progress – the sense that we are moving forward in some aspect of our lives. But what fuels progress? One thing only – Change. Impermanence.

While sharing the essence of Buddha's teachings, the renowned Zen monk, author, and meditation master Thich Nhat Hanh beautifully explains in one of his mindfulness books:

"When you look at the nature of things with concentration, you discover that they are impermanent. Everything is constantly changing. Nothing has a permanent identity. This impermanence is not a negative thing. If things were not impermanent, growth would be impossible and manifestation would be impossible too. If things were not impermanent, you could not have children, and your children would never grow up. When you sow seeds, they would never be able to grow. Impermanence is the very heart of life. It makes life possible. Reject impermanence, and you reject life."

Change is inevitable. It does not seek permission, nor does it wait for convenience. It arrives unannounced – sometimes in our favor, sometimes in ways that challenge us beyond our comfort zone. Yet, history has shown that our survival depends on one crucial ability – adaptation. From the dawn of civilization to today's fast-paced digital era, we have thrived not by resisting change but by evolving with it.

The world around us is in a state of constant transformation. One day, you look around, and everything feels different. But the truth is, change doesn't happen overnight. It unfolds every single day, in ways so small that we often fail to notice. Progress is not a sudden leap; it is the sum of these ongoing shifts.

That doesn't mean change is always easy. It can be uncomfortable, disorienting, even painful. But resisting it only leads to stagnation – a state as harmful as still water breeding bacteria. A stagnant lifestyle, much like stagnant water, fosters decay, gradually eroding opportunities, creativity, and personal growth. Without change, we risk becoming trapped in cycles that drain our energy and potential, leaving us stuck without progress.

There are countless moments in life where we find ourselves struggling to accept change. It could be the challenge of communicating with our teenage kids, who suddenly seem like strangers in their own world. Or adjusting to a new boss whose leadership style is nothing like the one we were used to. Maybe it's relocating to a new city or even a new country because of a job opportunity. And in traditional Indian societies, it's the life-altering shift when a woman moves into her husband's home after marriage.

No matter where you look, change is everywhere. It sneaks into every corner of life, testing our patience, adaptability, and resilience. The real question is – are we fighting it or embracing it?

So, how do we embrace change instead of fearing it? By developing a mindful mindset. Mindfulness, being aware in the present moment, allows us to see change not as a threat but as an opportunity – to learn, to innovate, and to grow. Because in the end, change is not the enemy. It is the very essence of life. And when we learn to flow with it, we realize that progress and the happiness that comes with it was always waiting for us.

Whenever you sense change happening, or feel it approaching, Accept and Adapt mindfully. That is the only way forward. Otherwise, you risk staying stuck in the past, caught in cycles of blame and regret, never truly moving ahead. Embrace impermanence, and you embrace life itself.

❖ ❖ ❖

"*Mindfulness is a way of befriending ourselves and our experience.*"
- Jon Kabat-Zinn

Why waste your life on guilt and regrets?

Maharpar was a kingdom of grandeur and wisdom, a land where the echoes of history merged with the vibrancy of progress. Nestled between vast golden plains and towering emerald hills, the kingdom stretched as far as the eye could see, its borders guarded by mighty rivers that shimmered under the sun's gaze.

At its heart lay the magnificent city of Rajagiri, home to the grand palace of King Chandrasen. The palace, an architectural marvel of towering domes and intricately carved sandstone pillars, stood as a testament to the kingdom's prosperity. The Darbar Hall, where wise ministers and scholars gathered, was adorned with murals that told stories of great battles, moments of wisdom, and the timeless pursuit of knowledge.

The streets of Maharpar were alive with the rhythm of trade and culture. Merchants from distant lands displayed their wares - silks from the east, spices from the south, and precious gems from the mines of the western mountains.

Poets and musicians filled the air with soulful verses and melodies, their voices mingling with the scent of sandalwood and jasmine that wafted through the busy bazaars.

Yet, Maharpar was more than its wealth and splendor. It was a land known for its people's intellect and discipline. Schools of astronomy and science flourished, where scholars debated the mysteries of the universe. Temples and meditation halls stood as sanctuaries for the seekers of spiritual enlightenment, their stone walls whispering ancient wisdom to those who paused to listen.

In the grand kingdom of Maharpar, there once ruled a wise and renowned king, Chandrasen. His wisdom was admired by all his people, neighbouring kings, and even his rivals. Chandrasen was decisive, a man who could solve the trickiest of dilemmas with ease. But sometimes, even the wisest of men falter, and it was an emotion, one single emotion that unravelled Chandrasen's life.

One summer evening, the court buzzed with excitement. A learned man named Shridutt had arrived. Shridutt was not just any scholar; he was known for his deep knowledge of the sciences, secrets of the universe, and the workings of the cosmos. King Chandrasen, a man of curiosity, was eager to meet him.

"The darbar shall assemble tonight," the king ordered, his eyes gleaming with anticipation.

As the sun set, the court gathered. Shridutt entered, and the entire darbar echoed with praises and hail. Dressed in simple robes, the scholar stood tall, unassuming yet commanding.

He began reciting poetry that unravelled the mysteries of the universe. His words painted vivid pictures of the stars, the planets, and the forces that moved them.

"How does the Earth spin, O learned one?" asked a courtier.

Shridutt smiled, his eyes twinkling like the stars he spoke of. "The Earth spins because of forces far greater than us, forces that bind the universe together in harmony," he explained.

Another voice from the court chimed in, "And how many planets are there in this vast universe?"

With a serene smile, Shridutt elaborated on his scientific observations, weaving his words with a calm confidence. The entire court was spellbound. Even King Chandrasen, who had never met a man of such profound knowledge, sat in stunned silence.

When the applause finally died down, the king rose from his throne. "Shridutt, dine with me tonight. We have much to discuss."

Later that night, under the soft glow of lanterns, Chandrasen and Shridutt sat in a private tent, a shamiana, indulging in a feast fit for kings. But the food was not what excited the king. It was the conversation.

"Tell me, Shridutt," the king began, leaning forward, "What do you think of the future of scientific growth in our world? Should we embrace it fully?"

Shridutt's eyes sparkled. "Science, O King, is not separate from life. It is in everything we do. Understanding the universe is the key to unlocking our future."

Chandrasen was enchanted by every word, every idea Shridutt spoke of. As the night wore on, the king decided to honour his guest. He presented Shridutt with a diamond-studded necklace, a token of admiration.

"With all due respect, my King," Shridutt said softly, "I live by knowledge and passion, not by wealth or adornment. I cannot accept this."

But Chandrasen insisted. "This necklace is not just a gift, Shridutt. It is a symbol of my respect for your wisdom. Please, accept it."

Reluctantly, Shridutt accepted, bowing deeply before leaving the palace.

The next morning, as Shridutt made his way out of the kingdom, a figure lurked in the shadows. A man, desperate and greedy, followed him. Just as Shridutt reached the outskirts, the man sprang forward, eyes wild, and attempted to snatch the scholar's bag.

"Stop! What are you doing?" Shridutt cried, but fear seized him. In the scuffle, the man stabbed Shridutt, not once, but three times. The scholar collapsed to the ground, his life slipping away. The necklace, still in his possession, lay bloodstained beside him.

News of Shridutt's murder reached the palace quickly, spreading like wildfire. King Chandrasen's heart filled with fury and anguish.

"Find the killer!" he roared. "And hang him at once!"

The culprit was caught and executed the same day. Justice, swift and cold, was served, yet King Chandrasen found no solace in it. In the days that followed, a gnawing unease clung to him like a shadow that would not fade. The image of Shridutt's lifeless body haunted him. It's my fault… the thought whispered endlessly in his mind. If I hadn't given him that necklace…

At first, it was a subtle discomfort, a quiet voice that he tried to ignore. But as the days passed, that voice grew louder, more relentless, echoing through his every waking moment. Chandrasen found no escape from it. The guilt, sharp as a blade, cut deeper with each passing hour. It wasn't just the idea that Shridutt had died, it was the unbearable belief that he, the king, was the reason.

What if I hadn't insisted? What if I had kept the gift to myself? Chandrasen's mind churned, replaying the moment again and again, every detail replayed in painful clarity. The glint of the diamond necklace. Shridutt's hesitant acceptance. The king's proud smile. That same necklace, now stained with blood, felt like a noose around Chandrasen's soul.

He could no longer sleep. When he closed his eyes, the nightmare of Shridutt's murder played on repeat, the faceless attacker and the scholar's final breath tormenting him in the dark. His bed, once a place of rest, now felt like a cage of guilt, trapping him in a spiral of regret. The weight of his conscience pressed heavily on his chest, suffocating him.

Food lost its taste. The lavish feasts that once brought him pleasure now seemed mangled. Each bite tasted like ash, each sip turned to dust in his mouth. Chandrasen, once strong and full of life, grew thinner with each passing day. His robes hung loosely on his frame, his eyes sunken and haunted.

Soon, he turned to drink, hoping the wine would numb the ache that festered within him. But the more he drank, the deeper the sorrow dug in. The wine blurred his vision but sharpened his inner torment, bringing out the worst of his thoughts. He drank to forget, but the alcohol only magnified the voices in his head.

"What kind of king are you?" he muttered to himself, stumbling through the halls of his palace, his voice thick with intoxication and self-loathing. "You should've known… you should've protected him!"

Chandrasen, once a pillar of wisdom and dignity, now became a shadow of his former self, staggering through his days, cursing the very air he breathed. His despair seeped into the kingdom like a poison. The once lively court grew silent, the people's spirits dimmed, and the energy of Maharpar dulled. Word spread quickly, The king has fallen.

And just as their king's heart grew heavy with guilt, so too did the kingdom's morale sink into the depths of despair. Without Chandrasen's steady hand, everything collapsed, the palace, the people, and even the land itself seemed to wither under the weight of his remorse. Guilt, a cruel and insidious emotion, had taken hold, and it would not let go.

The queen, desperate, called for a scholar and doctor known for his unconventional methods. "Cure him," she pleaded. "Restore our king."

The doctor arrived and, after examining Chandrasen, spoke quietly to the queen, "I can help the king… but only momentarily."

The court was puzzled. What good was a temporary cure? But they had little choice; the kingdom was crumbling under Chandrasen's torment.

When the doctor met the king, he whispered, "I have a power, O King. I can bring Shridutt back to life."

The king, delirious with excitement, blinked in disbelief. "Can you truly? Can you bring him back?"

The doctor nodded. "Yes, but there is a condition. I can bring only one person back. Shridutt... or the robber."

Chandrasen's excitement faltered. "The robber? Why would I want him back?"

The doctor's gaze was steady. "Justice, O King. If Shridutt lives again, the robber's punishment would be unjust. After all, he would not have committed murder."

A heavy silence filled the room. Chandrasen looked down, his hands trembling. "Then... bring neither back," he whispered. "I would achieve nothing by bringing Shridutt back if the robber is not here to face the same justice."

The doctor smiled. "Precisely, O King. Everyone must face their own destiny. You cannot control the fates of others, nor can you carry the weight of their actions. Guilt is but an emotion, it doesn't dictate anyone's destiny. You must let it go."

The king, for the first time in months, looked up with clarity. He walked to his closet, took out the diamond necklace, and without hesitation, threw it out of the window. It gleamed in the air for a moment before disappearing into the night.

As the wind blew through the room, Chandrasen smiled. "I feel... relieved," he murmured. "With this necklace gone, so is my guilt."

The doctor watched him and softly added, "Momentarily, O King. Momentarily."

(This story is inspired by an anonymous source. We do not claim any copyright or credits for it.)

Mindful Reflections: 》》

Guilt is surely an uncomfortable low-vibe emotion we all face when we believe our actions or words have hurt someone. While it can be a legitimate response - perhaps we made a mistake, said something we shouldn't have, or failed to act in a way that aligned with our values - it's essential to explore the root of that guilt. Often, it arises from not understanding and respecting our own principles or going against our beliefs. Sometimes, it arises when others point fingers, suggesting we haven't met their expectations.

Once guilt takes hold, self-doubt creeps in, and with it, our confidence begins to diminish. This emotional disturbance triggers the release of cortisol, a stress hormone that can weaken us both mentally and physically, creating a cycle that further entangles us in feelings of not eing enough.

What often follows guilt is regret, and isn't regret always tied to the past? When we dwell on our mistakes, replaying situations in our minds, it keeps us stuck in sadness. We cannot change what happened, but we often let guilt anchor us in those past moments, holding us back from growth and peace.

But here's something that could be done - what if, instead of being consumed by guilt, we become aware of it? What if we pause and ask ourselves, why do I feel this way? and what triggered this emotion? By being mindful of this emotion - guilt as it arises, we can begin to untangle its grip on us. The more aware we are the lesser grip this low-vibe emotion will have on us.

The truth is, no magic can erase guilt instantly. The only way forward is through self-awareness – staying present in the moment, trusting ourselves, and making the best decisions with the knowledge we have. Living in 'awareness mode' allows us to break free from the stagnation guilt brings, helping us heal, grow, and move forward.

Isn't it time to live this one life free from the heavy burden of guilt?

Take a moment to reflect on the regrets and guilt you may have been carrying for months or even years. Wake up to the reality that this low-vibration emotion doesn't just weigh on your mind – it can manifest in your body, leading to physical sickness. Many illnesses have arisen from unresolved mental burdens, so why wait to suffer when you can choose to heal now?

Sit with your regrets, explore them, and allow yourself to find the answers that will set you free – just like a deep exhale, releasing negativity from your mind and body. What is it that you feel guilty about?

What regrets are still lingering within you?

Is it about something harsh you once said?

A missed opportunity that you blame yourself for?

Do you believe that what happened is entirely your fault?

Now ask yourself – can you change the past? Is it something within your control?

And most importantly, what can you do right now to transform your actions moving forward?

Just take a deep breath in... and let it go. You've got this!

❖ ❖ ❖

"The past is gone, the future is unknown. What we have is this moment. Live it fully." - Prem Rawat

Jealousy is natural but not necessary

In the celestial realms where time flowed like an endless river of light, there was a voice that could make the heavens pause. It was said that when Tumbaru sang, the stars flickered in harmony, the winds stilled to listen, and even the gods themselves closed their eyes in rapture. His melodies were like golden threads woven into the fabric of the cosmos - smooth as honey, powerful as a tempest.

Born to Sage Kashyapa and Pradha, Tumbaru was no ordinary musician. His gift was a divine force, capable of stirring the souls of gods and mortals alike. Wherever his voice traveled, it left an imprint of wonder. Celestial beings whispered his name in reverence, and his praises echoed through the halls of Vaikuntha itself.

One day, on invitation by Lord Vishnu Himself, the divine sage Narada, the celestial messenger and devotee of Lord Vishnu, accompanied Tumbaru to Vaikuntha, the ethereal abode of the Supreme Lord. Narada, known for traversing the three worlds carrying divine wisdom and music, was a revered figure among the gods. As they entered, the air was filled with the fragrance of celestial blooms, and the soft luminescence of Vaikuntha's golden skies bathed them in its radiance. Tumbaru bowed before Lord Vishnu, his eyes gleaming with devotion. Then, with a deep breath, he began to sing. His voice carried the essence of surrender, flowing like waves brushing the shores of eternity. Each note resonated through Vaikuntha, melting into the very air. Lord Vishnu listened, eyes half-closed, a serene smile playing upon His lips, as if the universe itself had stilled to savor the music.

When the last note faded, silence reigned for a moment - profound, sacred before Lord Vishnu clapped His divine hands, the sound ringing like a blessing.

"Tumbaru," He said, His voice warm with delight, "your song is the breath of creation itself. It fills my heart with joy."

As a token of His pleasure, He gifted Tumbaru celestial ornaments that gleamed like the very stars.

Standing beside Tumbaru, Narada's heart clenched. His devotion to Lord Vishnu was unwavering, yet it was Tumbaru who received such divine praise! His fingers curled around his veena.

"I too shall please my Lord with song," he thought, determination burning within him. Yet beneath this resolve, a thorn of envy dug deep into his heart. The image of Tumbaru, basking in Vishnu's radiant smile, replayed in his mind, each note of the celestial musician's melody ringing like a cruel reminder of his own inadequacy.

With strong resolve, Narada lifted his veena and began to

sing. His voice, though drenched in devotion, lacked the depth, the richness, the celestial magic of Tumbaru's. The melody wavered, struggling to take flight. Lord Vishnu listened with kind patience, His expression unchanged.

A shadow of disappointment flickered across Narada's face. His heart ached. A slow burn spread within him - a frustration that festered into something darker. Why? Why did his song not stir the Lord's heart as Tumbaru's had? Was his devotion not pure enough? Was his love for Vishnu lesser than Tumbaru's?

Doubt twisted within him, turning his admiration for Tumbaru into a bitter rivalry. The sweetness of his devotion soured under the weight of comparison. His hands gripped his veena tighter, his chest tightening with an unfamiliar heaviness. The very air around him felt stifling, charged with the unspoken injustice of his failure. He was Narada, the celestial sage, the devoted messenger of the gods - how could he be anything less than the best?

Determined to silence the torment within, he left Vaikuntha and embarked on a journey to Mount Kailash, where Lord Shiva resided in deep meditation. Through searing winds and biting snow, through days that stretched into years, Narada performed severe penance. His body trembled from exhaustion, yet his spirit remained unyielding.

But even as he meditated, jealousy whispered in his ear, taunting him with the image of Tumbaru's effortless grace, the effortless love he seemed to receive. The more Narada yearned for perfection, the more his mind wove a tangled web of resentment.

At last, Shiva, the Lord of wisdom and arts, opened His

eyes. His voice, deep as the echoes of the cosmos, resonated through the mountains.

"Narada, what is it you seek?"

With folded hands and a voice trembling with longing, Narada spoke, "Mahadeva, bless me with the gift of divine music, so I may sing as beautifully as Tumbaru and please my Lord Vishnu."

Shiva gazed at him, his third eye gleaming with understanding. He saw the devotion, the desperation, and the festering jealousy that Narada himself refused to acknowledge. "So be it."

A wave of divine energy coursed through Narada. His voice grew smoother, his notes more refined, his melodies infused with newfound power. With a heart brimming with hope, he returned to Vaikuntha, eager to offer his song once more.

This time, his music was flawless - each note crisp, each rhythm precise. And yet... something was missing.

Lord Vishnu listened, His expression kind, yet untouched by the rapture that Tumbaru's song had evoked.

Doubt gnawed at Narada's soul. He roamed the heavens for thousands of years, practicing, refining, striving for the elusive perfection he sought. But no matter how much he improved, the divine joy remained just out of reach.

Weary and humbled, he finally sought Tumbaru. The celestial singer welcomed him with a warm smile, his aura calm as the gentle waves of a sacred river.

"Narada," Tumbaru said, "you seek to master music, but music is not merely sound. It is no comparison, its devotion, surrender, and love in its purest form. Allow me to guide you."

Narada, his jealousy now washed away by humility, bowed low. "Teach me, Tumbaru. I am ready to learn."

For years, Narada trained under Tumbaru, learning not just the mechanics of song but the soul of music itself. He realized that true melody did not reside in the perfection of notes, but in the offering of one's spirit through sound. Music was not a performance - it was a prayer.

When Narada finally returned to Vaikuntha and sang before Lord Vishnu in Dwarka, something miraculous happened.

His voice, no longer striving for grandeur, resonated with a divine purity. His song carried not the weight of competition, but the lightness of surrender. Each note flowed from his heart, unburdened, free.

Lord Vishnu closed His eyes, His very being covered with bliss. The melody enveloped Vaikuntha, shimmering like golden light upon still waters.

When the song ended, the Lord rose, His expression radiant. With infinite grace, He draped celestial robes upon Narada's shoulders and adorned him with shimmering ornaments.

"Narada," Vishnu said, "today, your song has truly reached my heart. It is not skill alone but the purity of devotion that makes music divine."

A slow, understanding smile spread across Narada's lips. The truth was clear at last - music was not meant to be conquered. It was meant to be surrendered.

With his veena in hand and his heart light as the wind, he continued his eternal journey, singing the praises of the divine across the cosmos - not to prove himself, but to offer himself.

And in that surrender, his music became truly eternal.

(This story is inspired by an anonymous source. We do not claim any copyright or credits for it.)

Mindful Reflections: 》》

"Jealousy is like drinking poison and hoping for the other person to die." This quote, often attributed to various thinkers, captures the self-destructive nature of envy. Yet, jealousy is an emotion every human being experiences at some point. It arises naturally, sometimes uninvited, like a shadow lurking in the mind when we are not always aware. The key, however, is not to suppress or ignore it but to accept it first and then transform it into a tool for growth and self-awareness. The more we accept our emotions (which are generated very naturally within us) the more easily you could become comfortable with those agonizing and low-vibe emotions, as let's not forget even the biggest iceberg is also a part of water, it's not a separate entity.

The next time you feel a pang of jealousy, pause and reflect. Ask yourself - What exactly am I jealous of? Is it someone's success, confidence, lifestyle, recognition, relationships they enjoy or perhaps their sense of purpose? Identifying the root of jealousy is the first step toward neutralizing its toxicity.

Once you pinpoint the object of your envy, separate the person from the thing they possess. Jealousy often conflates the two, making us resent individuals rather than acknowledging our own unfulfilled desires. For example, if you envy a colleague's career advancement, it's not the individual but the achievement that triggers the emotion. Recognizing this distinction shifts your focus from bitterness toward constructive action.

Now comes the most crucial step - channeling jealousy into motivation. Instead of letting it fester, use it as a signal pointing you toward aspirations you may not have fully acknowledged. Research, strategize, and take small steps toward acquiring that skill, opportunity, or mindset that you admired in someone else. By doing so, jealousy ceases to be a poison and instead becomes a roadmap toward self-discovery eventually leading to personal and professional fulfillment.

At its core, jealousy is a messenger, although an uncomfortable one. It reveals our hidden desires and unmet goals. Instead of drowning in it, use it as a catalyst to create the life you admire in others. After all, the energy you spend envying someone could be better invested in building your own success story, makes sense?

Accept your emotions - that is the core message of mindfulness. Embrace them with awareness and allow them to transform you. Every emotion, even jealousy, holds the potential to serve a greater purpose - if only we choose to view it as a guide rather than a burden.

❖ ❖ ❖

About The Author

Shweta Kulkarni, born in 1980 and raised in Mumbai - India, now resides in Pune with her husband and daughter. Originally educated as an architect, Shweta followed her passion and began her journey as a Zumba Instructor in 2011 that's where her holistic fitness journey began. Her dedication and talent led her to become a Zumba Education Specialist (ZES), and today, she serves as the LEAD Education Specialist for Zumba in India, focusing on leadership and strategy as a Professional Trainer and Speaker.

A passionate advocate of mindfulness and intentional living, Shweta leverages her expertise in wellness, mindfulness, and leadership to inspire individuals to cultivate balanced and purposeful lives. With over a decade of experience, she has empowered thousands of professionals through Licensed Zumba Instructor Trainings, ICF-certified Mindful Lifestyle Coach workshops, personal coaching sessions, and corporate employee wellbeing retreats. Her distinctive approach seamlessly blends evidence-based practices with relatable insights, making her teachings impactful and accessible to a wide range of audiences.

Beyond the classroom, Shweta is a Content Creator, Podcaster, Writer, and an occasional YouTuber. Her engaging narratives and practical wisdom resonate deeply with her audience, encouraging growth and self-discovery. Her debut book, Pause and Reflect - The First Volume of Mindful Lifestyle Blueprint for the Modern World, reflects her passion for promoting harmony and mindfulness in today's fast-paced world.

When she isn't teaching or writing, Shweta enjoys connecting with nature, traveling, reading, drawing and coloring Mandala designs, and continuously upgrading herself to reach her fullest potential in all aspects of life.

You can connect with Shweta at pauseandreflect2025@gmail.com.

Youtube - Shweta Kulkarni Studio

Instagram - @shwetaskul

Website - www.shwetakulkarni.com

List of my favourite books - Must Read

Hear Yourself - by Prem Rawat

You can heal your life - By Louise Hay

What are you doing with your life? - By J.Krishnamurti

Positivity, Confidence, Resilience, Motivation - By Paul Mckenna

Peace is every step - By Thich Nhat Hanh

Manifest - By Roxie Nafousi

Beyond The Pitch - By Dr. Divya Jaitly

Million Dollar Habits - By Brian Tracy

Being Nobody, Going Nowhere - By Ayya Khema

Mindfulness - By Ellen Langer

Family Wisdom - By Robin Sharma

You are here - By Thich Nhat Hanh

Atomic Habits - By James Clear

Stay Connected!

I would love to hear your thoughts and feedback about Pause and Reflect. Please feel free to reach out to me at pauseandreflect2025@gmail.com.

As a token of my mindful appreciation, every reader who leaves an Amazon review will receive a special gift from me. Simply send me the link or screenshot of your review shared on Amazon, along with your personal email address and I'll make sure to send something your way!

For more information about my work, upcoming projects, and to stay connected, visit www.shweta kulkarni.com.

Thank you for being part of this journey!

9 798897 246892